Minerals and Ancient Monuments in Royal Deeside

...links to our past

by Ian Cameron

Dedicated to Margaret,
who made this book possible.

FastPrint Publishing

www.fast-print.net/store.php

MINERALS AND ANCIENT MONUMENTS
IN ROYAL DEESIDE

Many thanks to Hugh Stewart for his help and advice during the preparation of this book.

Most photographs reproduced in this book were taken by the author. Others have been collected over the years and their sources are now unknown - the author hopes he may be forgiven if copyright has been unintentionally infringed.

Second edition published by Fast-Print Publishing of Peterborough, England

A catalogue record for this book is available from the British Library

ISBN 978-178035-699-0

Introduction

This book is the tale of my many excursions into the Deeside hills. I have been fortunate in that the nature of Castle Plant's work in forestry and on high ground has given me privileged access to many special places. The book also gained from the result of the discussions and revelations that followed these trips when we had regained the valley floor and friendly hostelries.

This book is also about people; family that felt the need to accompany me to the hills when I embarked on my more ambitious expeditions, folk that learnt me to 'keek' and read the ground and others whose company on the hill was reward enough in itself, like the three generations of Flat Coated retrievers and inquisitive Cairn terriers.

Through our work re-instating the quarried out flank of the Tomnaverie Stone Circle's hill at Tarland I made contact with a new set of professionals; the archaeologists probing Tomnaverie's secrets.

Along with Professor Richard Bradley from Reading University, who supervised the dig, I met Adam Welfare of the Royal Commission on the Ancient and Historical Monuments of Scotland, whose '*Great Crowns of Stone: The Recumbent Stone Circles of Scotland*' is the definitive work in its field. Adam Welfare and I had been researching the Recumbent Circles at the same time, yet quite unknown to each other until his book came out in 2011. Adam read my draft work and kindly agreed to write the foreword for this book.

Tomnaverie Circle continued to work its magic: at one of Avril's ceilidhs at the Coilacreach Inn, Paul Anderson joined in the music; and at the end of the evening I found a Strathspey called 'Tomnaverie' in his book of fiddle music compositions. Paul was so inspired by the Stones that he had composed this tune there. Paul was kind enough to allow me to re-produce the music sheet in this book.

Finally, this book was written in response to many requests to bring together my knowledge of the minerals and ancient monuments that can be found in Upper Deeside, and with the help of so many friends and sources, it is now complete. Enjoy.

Ian Cameron
Abergairn, 20/7/2013.

Foreword

Almost twenty years ago, my colleagues and I at the Royal Commission on the Ancient and Historical Monuments of Scotland, embarked upon a detailed survey of the field archaeology of the Don valley. Week after week we would journey north from Edinburgh, sometimes up the main road through Strathmore, the Mearns and the Mounth if working in the eastern lowlands, but at other times via Perth, Glen Shee and Braemar to the Dee, where we would turn east towards Ballater beside one of Britain's loveliest rivers.

This was the route to be preferred at any time of year. Perhaps best of all was the autumn when the leaves of the oaks, the birches and all the other deciduous trees would turn variously through yellow, orange and russet to fire-red in a display that cannot be matched elsewhere in the country. But winter was equally beguiling, because then the majestic mist-wreathed Scots pine of the Ballochbuie Forest could be glimpsed across the sparkling waters climbing high towards the broken ridges of snow-capped Lochnagar - a transient vision of the legendary Caledonian forest.

Often we would stop for sandwiches in Ballater, which, with its solid granite buildings, wide-open spaces and Royal warrants gaily displayed above almost every shop-front, is surely one of Scotland's prettiest small towns. If we were late we would divert through the narrow pass to the north and head off from Cambus O' May for Tarland and Alford, or instead follow the road up Glen Gairn in the direction of Corgarff or Strathdon. But whichever route was taken it was always clear from the diverse traces of glaciation, from the prehistoric hut-circles, the old enclosures, the clearance cairns, the quarries, the kilns, the old roads and the farmsteads still falling into ruin, that this striking landscape, with Ballater nestling at its heart like a gem, had many stories that remained untold.

Despite the proximity of Balmoral and the surpassing fame of the river, this is a country that still holds its secrets close and which even now are known only to a few. Ian Cameron, blessed alike in his place of birth and in the natural curiosity this has inspired, is the ideal guide. His knowledge is second to none. Moreover, he writes in a manner that is so free and so easy that the reader is soon running like a child through the town, across the haughs of the flood-plain and into the hills, which with their wooded mantles, their steep rocky outcrops and the moors stretching far above hide so many of the time-worn indicators that are witness to the activities of man in the past

However, first and foremost this is a landscape of stone, and it was the rocks with their signature minerals that so often drew people hereabouts. The ability to discover and extract these before putting them to good use is one of the main threads running through this book. And there is a strong autobiographical element, for even as a child they fascinated; and when much later the author felt impelled to collect and study them, he did so with a characteristic thoroughness. But that was not all he collected, because this is a book rich in anecdotes. Anecdotes about the beautiful agates that formed in the local basaltic lavas at unimaginable temperatures; the rare blue cairngorms found somewhere in the neighbourhood of Loch Builg; the opening of the mines for galena in Glen Gairn; the discovery of silver and perhaps even traces of gold; the veins of zinc, copper and tin; red garnets and the insistent search after limestone which could be burned using the local peat and then spread out on the fields to improve their fertility; the great quarries for granite in the Pass of Ballater and at Cambus O' May; and the quartz whose local characterisation as a 'good luck' stone may have its origin deep in prehistory, when the mineral appears to have been linked with the sun in order to represent the life force.

Yet there is so much more. Having worked for the Forestry Commission in Perthshire in his youth, the author shows a keen interest in the woodland scenery. He explains the importance of Joseph Farquharson's nursery, which was established at Monaltrie in the late 18th century, and provides a vivid account of the 'moving forest' of larch that has its origin in a planting near the bridge on the military road in Glen Gairn, but which has since spread much more widely. Indeed, change is a constant theme, whether this arose from the whims of the local landowners, or resulted from more impersonal forces impelled by events further afield.

The large numbers of archaeological sites and monuments around Ballater are testaments to the constancy of change. Many of these remains are little known to the wider world, and most, like the possible stone circle at Corrybeg, have yet to be evaluated in modern times; but these, too, have their stories. The author relates how Alexander Keiller, whose great wealth was founded upon the famous Dundee marmalade, conducted an exploratory excavation at Corrybeg, having first spotted the site from the air. He is also said to have undertaken another on the Coyles of Muick and on this occasion he apparently buried a sealed container preserving a record of his findings. These are memories that are now held only locally, but it is a reminder that Keiller's great love of the past was also nurtured in these hills. And just as Britain came to owe him a debt of gratitude for the partial excavation and restoration of the great stone circle at Avebury, so it also owes him a similar debt for pioneering and financing the new technique of aerial photography. This was not only to lead to such important discoveries as the western extension of the Stonehenge Avenue, but also to the recovery of thousands of sites of all periods throughout the length and breadth of the country. This same debt is also owed to his native land.

The author recounts all these stories with great flair, while the quality of his photography and the sheer number of images is an additional pleasure. The great care with which these have been integrated with the text adds immeasurably to the attractiveness of the book.

Many readers who are relatively unfamiliar with the area will sometimes find it helpful to have a current Ordnance Survey map to hand; and for those occasions when the author writes of earlier times, we are fortunate to live in a digital age, for previous editions at a wide range of scales reaching back to the mid-1860s are now freely accessible online through the website of the National Library of Scotland. In addition, applications like Google Earth can be used to reveal the actual character of the landscape, while sometimes additional information about the ancient archaeological sites, the ruined farms, the abandoned mines, the quarries and much more may be found on the Canmore website of RCAHMS. However, this area has not been the subject of an intensive study like that centred on Donside.

This fascinating book invites the reader to explore an exhilarating landscape. Yet the author is such an affable and engaging guide that it would be a dull soul indeed who could resist the call to examine the granites in the Pass of Ballater, in order to discover beryl, topaz, tourmaline and purple amethyst, or scout out the 'hidden valley' above Creag an t-Seabhaig. There are also the shieling grounds of Easter Morven, the 'elvan dyke' near Corrybeg and the great stag that is sometimes to be seen outlined in the snows below Lochnagar. And who would not wish to visit the recumbent stone circle at Tomnaverie, in order to appreciate the author's theory, or perhaps venture further north to Auchmaliddie, where the great recumbent stone and the one surviving flanker of pure, gleaming white quartz once led Keiller to declare that this ring, when originally complete, 'must have presented a spectacle unparalleled for impressiveness'? Admittedly, this lies much further afield, but closer to hand are the 'upside down' stone at Rinabaich, the ringing stone at Richarkarie, the lead mines of Abagairn, the site of the Newfoundland lumberjacks' camp, and many more of the locations that are referred to in this evocative and memorable book.

Adam Welfare

Stannington, Northumberland (17 March 2013)

CHAPTER 1.

Minerals and Ancient Monuments... links to our past

Romancing the stones

The Ballater that I grew up in was a granite town; the square-set streets with granite-kerbed pavements were bounded by granite rubble walls, granite houses, granite halls, granite kirks and a massive granite bridge. The world is granite, I deduced.

There was something magic about my granite; it was exciting to walk on and felt so alive under my feet. The familiar texture, too was reassuring, and has always made me feel comfortable and at 'home'.

On our boyhood expeditions, we used to take the 'cinder pathie' from the Cricket Park, as we knew it but now known as the Monaltrie Park, to the Pass of Ballater. This 'pathie' was resurfaced regularly with cinders from the fireboxes of the Deeside railway engines, hence the name. Time had proved the cinders to be a very suitable material for that purpose.

We walked past the front of Monaltrie House, pausing to inspect the progress of that year's maturing crop of conkers growing spikily from the boughs of the great chestnut trees that lined the east drive, before we set off down the Pass.

We headed up a steep path, skirting the remains of the camp where the first Newfoundlanders had lived when they were clearing the trees off the lower slopes of Creag an t-Seabhaig in World War Two, and climbed carefully on to where you can get a view of ruined Tullich Kirk, and, looking straight down, can see the outdoor rifle range built along the east bank of the Tullich Burn. If red warning flag was not flying we were safe to keep climbing up the road.

A little further up the road, as we headed north for Morven and turned our back on the Dee valley and our bird's eye view of Pannanich Wells Hotel on the opposite bank of the river, something happened, you can feel it in your bones: we had suddenly lost our granite.

As we carried on, the road swung steeply to the left and we were near the top of the hill. The rocks around us looked strange, no longer magic, and quite

The first Newfoundlanders'camp on the Pass of Ballater. © Ian Cameron

rusty. The road now swung back on itself and on our left was an old quarry. The area around it is unnaturally flat and green, vivid green against the heather: beneath that platform was a man-made stone structure, but the stones had changed now to blue/grey.

The stone structure was a lime kiln, built into the slope beneath the lime quarry to allow easy loading from the top and also to provide up-draught

The lime kiln beneath the quarry and latter-day mast buildings. © Ian Cameron

when alight. That was where the quarried limestone was burned into lime, and then carted down the road we had just climbed to be spread on the lime-starved fields along the Dee below.

This photo pre-dates the trees that cover the site today.

Close by the quarry is a lochan set on the hill top. This had formed as the old quarriers dug out the peat to fuel their kiln; one layer of limestone, one layer of peat, repeated again and again until the barrel-shaped structure was full. The kiln was set alight: it would burn for days, after which the powdered lime would be raked out of a hole in the bottom of the kiln, and carted away to improve fields at the time of the improvements, in Deeside's case, late 18th Century, early 19th Century.

That gave us lots to think about; our granite was not as omni-present as we had thought! Its very solidity was now suspected.

In fact, the granite hills, to the north of Ballater and the immediate Dee valley, soon gave way to older rocks, gabbros, hornsfelds and limestone that ran to the top of Morven Hill and beyond, giving Easter Morven its lush green grass each June.

This is where Neolithic man planted his early crops. Still to be seen are his corn kilns, hut circles, wells and enclosures.

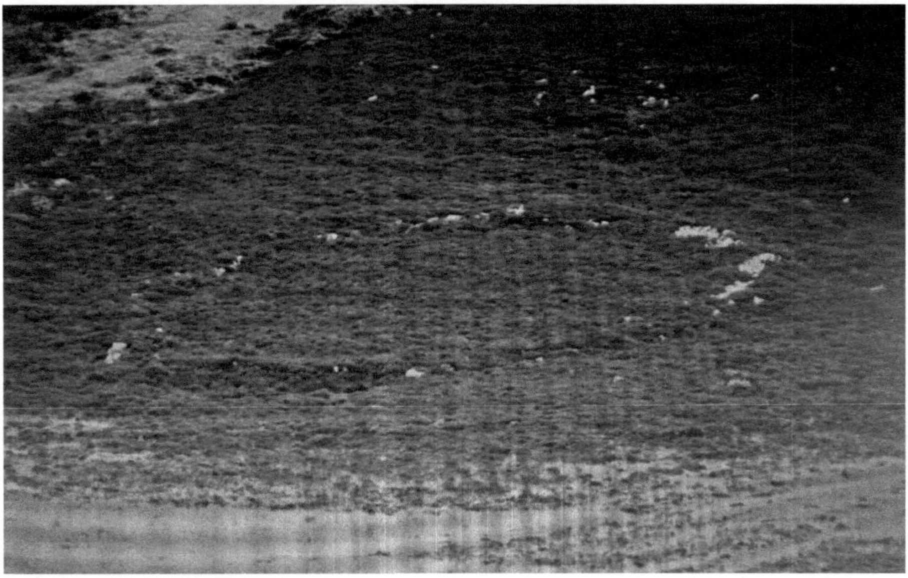

Early enclosures. © Ian Cameron

Old habits die hard, and, well into the 19th Century, the Tarland folk used to take their cattle to the shielings on Easter Morven for the summer grazing.

We boys scrambled back to the very top of Creag an t-Seabhaig and walked on a network of quartz veins criss-crossing the exposed rock. That host rock was a mix of the old Morven gabbros cut by the younger Ballater granite. The veins were mostly cloudy quartz, but here and there little crystals of yellow citrine could be found, dog-tooth quartz and calcite crystals abounded.

The network of quartz veins. © Ian Cameron

What we had found was the contact area between the older rocks and the more recent 350-million-year-old granite. Those contacts always threw out minerals and, although we did not understand the reasons, we stored away memories of where we found special rocks.

As we walked back down the track, we took time to look more closely at the rusty rocks. They were ironstone and carried small yellow cubes of 'fool's gold', iron pyrites; other rocks were stained quite yellow and covered, we noticed, by a filigree of silver-coloured metallic encrustations (*See colour plate 1*).

You can trace this seam of sulphide mineralisation all the way from Glen Girnoc; it crosses the Dee, outcropping strongly at the lead mines of Abergairn, and then continuing up past Balmenach and beneath the TV mast on top of Creag an t-Seabhaig before disappearing at the Tullich burn where it gets lost under the more recent granites of Crannich Hill.

The limestone on Tom an Lagain. © Ian Cameron

Seams of limestone are to be found in association with that mineralisation: apart from the quarry and kiln on Creag an t-Seabhaig, the old folk quarried lime on Tom an Lagain just south of the summit of Creag Phiobaidh in Glen Girnoc. A cart track leaves the B 976, runs past Loch Ullachie and round the shoulder of Creag Liath to reach this quarry.

The efforts the Upper Deeside farmers made to seek out the elusive seams of lime never fail to amaze me, time and again I find their early trial pits deep out in the mountains.

Another lime quarry is to be found on Tom Meann just below the lead mines at Abergairn. To serve that quarry, there was built a magnificent lime kiln: you can see it to this day behind the old Free Church Manse of Craggan, just off the Pass of Ballater. This kiln is far too well-preserved to have had a long working life: not long after it was completed, the railway reached Ballater. That spelt the end for local lime production as lime companies opened offices and stores at all the Deeside railway stations and supplies of cheap English lime steamed in to meet the farmers' carts.

Lime kiln at Craggan. © Ian Cameron

As time passed by, I left my granite, first for Germany's plains, then Perthshire and Fife's great variety of hills, fields and forests, where, out of the blue, revelation came.

CHAPTER 2.

A gateway to a new World

Forestry Commission days in Glen Devon

One day, as I was walking back down the Glen, I saw the District Officer from the Perth Office coming up the hill towards me. Every now and then, he stopped and picked something out of the ditch of the new forest road that we were constructing. As we met, I asked him what he was doing. 'Collecting agates,' said he; and for me a new world was born. Up till that moment of time, a stone was a stone: from that time on, there were no such things as stones, only an infinite variety of minerals.

The agates the D.O. collected were the solidified gases of minerals that had formed in cavities in the host basaltic lavas, and were now being released by our mechanical labours, rather than the usual slow erosion of frost, wind and rain.

He showed me his afternoon's collection of beautiful, multi-coloured, banded stones. I spent the rest of the day puddling in the mud; then couldn't get home to Margaret quickly enough to show her my treasure and share with her my new knowledge (*See colour plate 2*).

That started me on a search for information on agates, or Scotch Pebbles as they used to be known. The Victorians had been very keen on agates, and they are found in most antique Victorian jewellery. The Victorians were much more mineral-conscious than we are today, they were living in an age of mining coal and minerals, and at a time of limestone quarries and iron mines - all the land-based industries that had made Britain great, and the Clyde the workshop of the world.

A Dr Heddle, of Arcadian origin, wrote the definitive 'Mineralogy of Scotland'. In it, he explores mines, mountains, quarries and railway cuttings, anywhere he could get at bedrock to search for new minerals. Dr Heddle had a special love for agates, and his collection may be seen in the Museum of Scotland in Edinburgh.

The Victorians had also a great interest in Cairngorm crystals, perhaps fed by Victoria's extended mourning, as the Cairngorms dark and broody crystals made ideal mourning jewellery. Indeed, till the time of the Great War, jewellers' shops, in Ballater and Braemar, specialised in mounting local cairngorms crystals in silver for that very purpose.

Anyhow, overnight, I became a 'rock hound.' I trailed Margaret and our young family all over Scotland searching for the elusive gems; and as the collection grew, I bought and constructed gem-polishing machines, diamond saws to slice up the agates, and laps to shape and finish the stones (*See colour plate 3*).

A lapidary club was formed in Dunkeld, and our Instructor was Wattie Muir. Wattie had been a lead-miner at Leadhills in Lanarkshire, working alongside his father, who, himself, had been a great authority on Scottish gold.

The Second World War came, the mines were closed, and Wattie went to work in an Edinburgh engineering works; there he lost an eye, while operating a drilling machine making parts for naval guns.

Wattie's job, by 1965, was creating ornaments out of Glen Tilt marble. The raw material, the marble, Wattie won from the bed of the River Tilt and then transported to his workshop in his faithful three-wheeled van. Wattie took the Dunkeld Club on visits to his Edinburgh Lapidary Club; the members there, mainly teachers and other professionals, all accepted Wattie's singular experience and enthusiasm, his advice being eagerly sought on identifying their latest finds. It was there that I saw my first geological maps of Scotland, and started to realise the complexity of our subject.

The whole world was reeling from the first Australian 'Poseidon' mineral boom: the geologists were going mad, and I suppose me with them.

Various mining companies were drilling holes all across the North East, trying to tie wary farmers down in royalty agreements: heavy minerals were the goal; platinum, tungsten, lead, copper and silver.

On Deeside, people were employed locally to search the beds of the burns, filling little bags with samples of gravel collected every 50 yards. Sometimes, when the geologists-in-charge thought they had found something sufficiently interesting, a helicopter was called in to air-lift the sample to a laboratory for chemical analysis. That happened on several occasions when the work was concentrating on burns coming off the western slopes of Morven Hill.

All that frenzied activity died with the collapse of Poseidon shares, and we all went back to our day jobs.

CHAPTER 3.

Lead not dead

Abergairn Lead Mine

My mad mineral phase led me back to Deeside and the 'special rocks' I remembered from boyhood. Deeside had no recent volcanic rocks, nor agates, but it made up for that with a seemingly infinite range of other minerals.

Our school friends; the Durward twins, Eric and Ian, had lived at Abergairn farm, and we were quite well acquainted with the lead mines behind their house. Years later, while attending College in Aberdeen as a mature student, I used to make ends meet by fabricating and erecting railings and gates all over Ballater. The fabrication was no problem; just cut the steel to length and weld it together. The scrolls were a different story.

In my Forestry Commission days in Perthshire, I used Alex Law's smiddy, outside Aberfeldy, for much of the heavy machinery repairs, and Alex crafted a former for me to make scrolls on. That former was no good without a forge, so I made a deal with Charlie Clark, the last blacksmith at the Bridge of Gairn smiddy. Charlie was semi-retired by 1970: he had stopped trying to keep up with a world that no longer needed horses. Our deal was: he would accept repairs all week, and I would bring my portable electric welder on Saturday mornings and weld his work first, then he would allow me the use of his forge to heat and shape the scrolls for my gates in the afternoons (*See colour plate 4*).

That arrangement worked well, and, together, we drank the many cups of tea that his sister endlessly brewed. Charlie loved to gossip and news, and one day I mentioned the many white quartz stones lying around the smiddy.

"They all came out of the lead mines," said Charlie.

We had heard at school that there was not enough lead to make it pay.

"Not a bit of it," said Charlie. "My father came fae the fit o' the Knock's brae, to take o'er this smiddy, just to cater for the miners and sharpen their tools."

"So why did it stop?" I asked.

"The auld Marquis (of Huntly) got into debt. He gambled a' the hours o' the nicht at Abergeldie Castle wi' the Prince of Wales; he first started selling wids (woods) then grun (ground)." "Finally he had to sell a' Morven Estate to Auld Keiller o' Dundee. But there was aye plenty o' good lead, the miners were not fit to lift a ful (full) shovel, and the deeper they dug the better it got. They even extended the railway line up frae Ballater to cairt it awa."

But the last thing John Mitchell Keiller wanted on his new sporting estate was industry, so the miners had to go.

The Welcoming Arch at Bridge of Gairn for King George V in 1911. © Ian Cameron

The Clark family are well represented in this photo. The white-bearded gent standing in the centre of the arch was Mr Clark, Senior, blacksmith, and doubtless the driving force for the construction of this structure. This is the father that Charlie Clark speaks of as having come to the Bridge of Gairn smiddy to cater for the lead miners. On the extreme right are the Clark family, two daughters and four sons. The Charlie Clark that I knew is the youngest son, sixth from the right.

Abergairn Lead Mine. © Ian Cameron

Years later, my good friend, the late Dr Mike Gallagher of the British Geological Survey, confirmed Charlie's story. He told me that, quite apart from the silver-bearing lead ore, Abergairn was a potential major source of fluorspar. The fluorite crystals of green, violet and blue are highly prized for jewellery and also for the new thinking of crystal healing, and it is used as a source of fluorine for the fluoro-chemical, steel and aluminium industries. Mike would then add, tantalisingly: "But don't forget the gold!"

Man has hunted for minerals around Abergairn for a long, long time. Bronze Age man then Iron Age man, who levelled the top of near-by Tom Meann to build on. Romans passed this way, en-route to their marching camps at Glen Fenzie and Allargue over on Donside. The Romans' remit in Scotland had nothing to do with territory and conquests, but everything to do with prospecting for, and acquiring, gold and silver to send back to Rome.

The remaining mine workings to be seen today consist of pits dug behind an ancient dyke at the top of the red park, with the actual spoil lying heaped against this wall. At the largest pit there is evidence of a sorting floor where the ores of zinc, fluorite and calcite, that were separated from the galena (lead ore), can still be found.

The mineral vein appears to be fault-guided and follows the line of the wall, in a roughly North-South direction; trials pits in the early 1800s had proved that the vein had several branches: at that time, it was believed to extend 120 yards. While excavating behind the Craggan house, 10 years ago, Castle Plant came on fluorite and galena in a vein at least 400 yards beyond, and 150 feet lower than, the old workings on the hill.

There is evidence of calcite, galena and zinc-blende in the spoil heaps from the earlier, extensive, shafts and trial pits on Tom Meann, and it would not be extravagant to claim that the mineralisation here is much more extensive than was ever thought of in the 1800s'.

Later on in the mid-1870s, Cornish miners, brought in by Lord Huntly's agent, drove a tunnel from the corner of the field beneath Abergairn farm house to drain the mine workings. That adit drains into an open ditch between fields to this day. Once the mine was dewatered, the miners drove an upper adit from Abergairn garden into the hill to intersect the vein at depth, and brought the ore out by rail track to tip and sort just west of our present home. In more recent times, a hole opened up in the Red Park and swallowed a calf; this was caused by the collapse of the roof of this tunnel from the weight of modern farm machinery.

The 'Elvan Dyke' extending over the Corrybeg burn and up on to Prony hill. © Ian Cameron

Beyond the workings, and stretching northward to the Corrybeg burn, is a ridge of rock; this exposure is particularly interesting as it is a quartz-feldspar porphyry dyke, the Elvan dyke beloved of the Cornish miners, their true-fire indicator of near-by mineralisation in Cornwall (*See colour plate 5*).

This dyke disappears at the Corrybeg burn, but, at times of light snow cover, a tell-tale depression, almost a ghost of the dyke, can be seen to carry on up the east side of Prony Hill as far as Fox's well.

Snow drift filling the depression above the mineral vein on Prony Hill. © Ian Cameron

The rock of this dyke contains large felspar crystals on a ground mass of smaller quartz crystals of great purity, mica and the haematite, which once eroded out, gives the Red Park below its colour and name.

CHAPTER 4.

Rock and roll shock

Pass of Ballater Silver Mine

We often climbed about in the Pass of Ballater: usually we were trying to reach the nests of the ravens, which still lived there in the 1940s. When the ravens defeated us, we would start looking for strange rocks. There was, and still is, a vertical mineral vein that runs up over the top of the cliff: this vein gave up many different crystals, lithium ores, green microcline, fluorite and beryl.

On a compass setting, that vein travels north to a hidden valley that had been an early run-off channel for the impounded glacial ice-melt waters trying to escape down-valley, at a time before the Pass of Ballater had been eroded out. The erosion there is still active today; in the spring of 2004 a huge mass of rock fell off the cliffs, the resultant shock waves being recorded by the British Geological Survey's instruments in Edinburgh.

Rock fall in Pass of Ballater. © Ian Cameron

The easiest way to reach this hidden valley from the Pass is by starting at the gate on the bridge at the Fog House. This was Francis Farquharson's work after he returned from exile in England following his exploits in the 1745 rising.

The Fog House was a folly built into the bank of the Loin burn that flows through the Pass. It would have been constructed at the same time as the bridge that gave access to the granite quarries on the hill above. Its name stems from the roofing of heather and fog (moss).

Farquharson's Monaltrie House was built in 1782 from the red granite that he quarried here.

Francis Farquharson's Fog House and bridge in the Pass of Ballater. © Ian Cameron

The early 1780s would have been a busy time in the Pass of Ballater quarries; apart from Monaltrie House stone, the first Ballater Bridge that opened to traffic in 1783 was being built from granite won here.

You can still follow the track, traversing the hill that accessed the various levels where Francis Farquharson quarried the building stone from large boulders on the steep scree slope.

Not only did Francis Farquarson use those quarries for the stones of Monaltrie House and Ballater's first bridge, but his successor, William Farquharson, built the original Monaltrie Arms Hotel, the farm buildings that went with the hotel, and most of the early houses of Bridge Square of this same rough red granite.

The shift to the Cambus o'May quarries came later, with the local masons leasing quarries there from the Marquis of Huntly, and so becoming contractors in their own right and able to supply their own stone independent of the local laird and his quarry.

The granite at Cambus o'May was also much finer grained than the red stone of the Pass and much easier to cut and dress.

The shift to the Cambus quarries did not please the Farquharson lairds at Invercauld House who had gained the Monaltrie estate on William's death.

After the railway reached Ballater in 1866, the Invercauld Estate was swamped with requests to buy building land in Ballater. The estate was quite happy to oblige, but with conditions attached, one demanding that the proposed house be built of granite won and paid for from the old quarries on Invercauld ground at the Pass of Ballater.

That monopoly on building stone meant that the rough red Pass of Ballater granite got a new lease of life, and explains how the vast majority of the houses continued to be built of that granite long after the Cambus quarries came into operation.

We have to wait until the Edwardian days, with their final boom of building, for the Cambus quarries really to come into their own, quite briefly as it happened, before the hard, white Kemnay granite came steaming up the valley on railway trucks to face the great villas we see today on Braemar and Queens Roads.

From a strictly minerals point of view, this seemingly endless exposure of rough red granite walls all around us in Ballater provides a most natural classroom.

One of the quarry levels. © Ian Cameron

I am reminded of John Betjeman on his first visit to Aberdeen, and I quote:

"No one can go to Aberdeen and not become interested in granite. I shall not forget my amazement, taking the tramcar one windy day down to the sea beach for the first time and standing on a lonely shore below the tufted links which separate Aberdeen from the sea. All around me was the veined and glittering produce of the cliffs of Scotland pounded into rounds and ovals by resistless breakers. So beautiful, so varied were the stones on the beach, grey, silver, pink, red, crimson, white, green, purple, pink-red, and silver again, that for a moment it was like standing in a dream of avarice surrounded by precious stones. And then, on the tide line where the waves had washed the pebbles so that they were still wet, they glowed with an intenser colour just as the city of Aberdeen glows deeper, richer silver after rain. I collected fifteen different sorts of granite in as many minutes."

My next photo shows a very typical backstreet dyke in Ballater, the variety of stones incorporated vying aesthetically with John Betjeman's discovery on Aberdeen beach (*See colour plate 6*).

The Pass of Ballater granite, for reasons I have just described, was being exhausted; the best stone had long gone and now faulted, veined and mineralised rock can be found in every wall. Look carefully and find quartz veins cutting the stones: there are flat mica plates, pointy quartz crystals, and blocky feldspar crystals as big as match boxes and, with a hand lens, you will find the pegmatite minerals of topaz, zircon, tourmaline, beryl and purple amethyst (*See colour plate 7*).

It is also interesting to note that, in the older houses, masons sometimes incorporated a single solid quartz stone into the walls for good luck. This tradition goes far back into the mists of time and is a continuation of the ancients' affinity with quartz, so apparent in the quartz chips found in their graves and stone circles (*See colour plate 8*).

That reminds us of the Snow Tower at Kildrummy Castle, built entirely out of quartz, and said to be almost vibrant in full-moon light. The Tower contained five floors of accommodation and was the owner's main residence until the Elphinstone tower was built in the 1500's.

The Snow tower collapsed, without warning, in 1805; locals maintained that its destruction was precipitated by an earth tremor and Kildrummy folk still swear that a white cloud of quartz dust rose from the debris and took the form of an Angel as it passed overhead and circled around before landing two miles away across the Don valley.

This building in quartz had a very early precedent; Alexander Keiller read a paper on the Megalithic Monuments of North-East Scotland at a Meeting of the British Association on September 7th, 1934, in Aberdeen. In his talk he describes most of the North-East stone circles, and I quote: "One cannot leave the subject of the petrology of these Stone Circles without further reference to the superb appearance of the white quartz outlier at Balquhain. To those, however, with an imaginative eye for these Circles as edifices of great beauty in themselves, I would strongly recommend a visit to the little-known remnants of the Circle of Auchmaliddie, where the only two Stones now remaining – the Recumbent and the right Pillar – are also of pure quartz, while from broken boulders in the adjacent dykes it would appear more than possible that the entire Circle may have been composed of this rock: in which case it must have presented a spectacle unparallel for impressiveness."

Time has not been kind to remains of Alexander Keiller's Circle at Auchmaliddie; on a recent visit we found that both Recumbent and Pillar had been uprooted, but such was the mass of the stones they had been left lying there on their hilltop sharing the great expanse of Buchan skyline and heaven with the new power technology of wind turbines.

There is no doubt that quartz has held a fascination for people down through the ages.

The Auchmaliddie quartz stones. © Ian Cameron

I have included a photo, from around 1880s, of ladies knitting outside an old house near Glascorrie. On the window sill behind them can be seen a collection of quartz stones, found, probably, in the quarries near-by.

The quartz collection. © Ian Cameron

On a more personal note, I found myself falling under the spell of Quartz, and when Castle Plant was asked to build a rubble wall to support a path outside the then brand new Craigendarroch Hotel extension, I could not resist incorporating a Quartz stone (*See colour plate 9*).

Let us never be flippant about quartz: remember that the oscillations of a tiny chip of quartz regulate every item of technology in our modern world.

I digress. As we continue up the track from the Pass road we find mature firs blocking the path of what had been the horse-and-cart track up to the quarries; almost two hundred years have passed and nature has been reclaiming her hill for a long time.

The track is built as steep as a horse could climb, but of one thing we can be sure, the return trip with a loaded cart of granite would have required a second horse chained behind to hold the load back till level ground was reached.

Once we reach the quarry level, there are still traces of the rough shelter where the masons lunched and doubtless sheltered from the worst of the weather.

The quarriers' shelter complete with anthill. © Ian Cameron

The granite here is very coarse with large crystals; indicating that it had cooled very slowly, allowing the constituent minerals, the micas, the feldspar and indeed the quartz crystals, to form individually.

Under such conditions, and in this locality, are found the Cairngorms crystals.

Continue past the quarry and carry on up the hill: soon you will come to the hidden valley (*See colour plate 11*).

At the entrance is a still recognisable ditch that drained the mine workings. It is note-worthy that the vegetation here has altered to that which will withstand the still highly toxic contents of the drain.

This ditch is deeper and longer than I had remembered; at the entrance is a huge mound of excavations won from the ditch.

The ditch dug to drain the mine workings. © Ian Cameron

I estimate that more than two hundred tons has been dug by pick and shovel and barrowed out of this cutting (*See colour plate 12*).

On your right is a sheer cliff face, with erosion scree-flows spilling from the bottom of the cliff to the valley floor. On your left are traditional Scots pine woodlands and a path that skirts the scree. Look again at the cliff face: there is a holly tree clinging, improbably, from the crags. Farther along is the mineral vein, ascending the face, the continuation of the ore vein we saw on the Pass, except that by now it is carrying lead ore. Climb out along the foot of the cliff; when you reach the lead ore vein follow it down into the scree.

In my youth, a mere one hundred and fifty years after Francis Farquharson's nephew, William, was conducting his mining operations, you could still see the rotting timbers that supported his shaft, following the vein deep into Creag an t-Seabhaig. The galena proved to be argentiferous, from the Latin argentum (silver). It was like Abergairn, silver-bearing lead ore.

It was William Farquharson's proud boast that he had recovered enough silver to have cast a set of silver buttons for his dress tunic (*See colour plate 10*).

Today you can no longer see the timbers, and 60 more years of erosion have tumbled many boulders down the scree slope into the shaft, but if you know where to look, the entrance can still be seen.

The entrance to the Mine shaft outlined. © Ian Cameron

Looking up at the rock face from the mine entrance. © Ian Cameron

The rocks in this scree are well worth examination for both mineral ores and crystals, amazingly so near Ballater yet so undisturbed

With evidence of much earlier mining at the cliff base

It is very interesting to note all the lead mining that was going on around here in the early days of the 19th Century. We see activity at Abergairn and at the Pass of Ballater. Meanwhile, on the south side of the Dee, the Gordon laird of Abergeldie was also mining away for lead on the exposed veins of Creag Ghiubhais.

The mineral veins on Creag Ghiubhais. © Ian Cameron

I digress a little; but one hundred and forty years later the 22nd/24th companies of the Canadian Forestry Corps came over to clear-fell the

Scots pine on Creag Ghiubhais during the Second World War. The Canadians could not believe the mineral wealth lying around unexploited. Those men were very mineral conscious; many had worked in mines in pre-war Canada, and saw here the potential for mining lead, zinc and silver. It was a topic in the local pubs all through the war.

Back to our tale; in the early 1800s, and by 1805 especially, we have to remember that Britain was fighting with France in the Napoleonic wars and an invasion of these islands seemed imminent.

The Glengarry Badge of the 5th Volunteer Battalion Ballater Company. © Ian Cameron

We read of local militias being formed, like the 5th Volunteer Battalion with its Ballater Company, and, whether through patriotism, or for monetary gain, many lead mines were opened throughout Scotland.

Lead was undoubtedly at a premium for bullets, and the great mines at Strontian, that General Wade had shares in from the 1720s',

Strontian Lead Mines. © Ian Cameron

were very busy. Strontian is situated at the head of Loch Sunart on the west coast; and many, many miles from Ballater, but as a major mineral location I have brought it into my book.

The minerals there were discovered around 1722; by 1724 the York Building Co. had acquired the mining rights. After the Union of the Parliaments, that organisation had acquired many timber concessions for pine, mainly on the Spey, and oak woods in Argyll to produce charcoal to smelt imported iron ore from Cumbria.

The York Building Co. saw the Strontian lead mines as yet another business opportunity, but a mineral deposit high on a remote mountain, with hostile Highlanders removing their supplies and even their cattle, caused the company to send an urgent request to General Wade for a detachment from his road-building troops to guard the mine. The good general complied, and, whether he thought it a good investment, or he was simply being rewarded for his protection, it is known that he acquired shares in the Company.

The Highlanders refused to work underground. 'It is a bad place', they said 'the home of evil spirits'. That Highland superstition could well have been based on much earlier health problems experienced at Strontian, but, as time passed, toxic radio-active minerals were identified in the mines. Indeed the element Strontium was first identified here, and named after the locality.

Labour then came from farther afield. The government brought in French prisoners-of-war. Those unfortunates were set to mining lead for bullets and artillery shells destined to be fired at their own countrymen all over the Continent, and, finally, and drastically so, at Waterloo.

Colour plate 1. *The Rusty Rocks.* © Ian Cameron

Colour plate 2. *Agate after cutting by diamond saw blade.* © Ian Cameron

Colour plate 3. *The writer's collection of Scottish semi-precious Gem-stones. © Ian Cameron*

Colour plate 4. *Charlie Clark and friend. © Ian Cameron*

Colour plate 5. *Quartz-feldspar porphyry.* © Ian Cameron

Colour plate 6. *Ballater back garden dyke.* © Ian Cameron

Colour plate 7. *Pegmatite vein running through granite stone. © Ian Cameron*

Colour plate 8. *Quartz Good Luck Stone. © Ian Cameron*

Colour plate 9. *The Quartz stone in the wall. © Ian Cameron*

Colour plate 10. *Argentiferous Galena (Silver-Lead ore). © Ian Cameron*

Colour plate 11. *The Hidden Valley. © Ian Cameron*

Colour plate 12. *The pile of excavations, much older than the pine trees that have grown on it.* © Ian Cameron

Colour plate 13. *The Old South Deeside Road beneath Pannanich.* © Ian Cameron

Colour plate 14. *The Borrow Pit for the March Dyke.* © Ian Cameron

Colour plate 15. *The Great Divide.* © Ian Cameron

Colour plate 16. *The Lady's Stone.* © Ian Cameron

Colour plate 17. *Flint and chalcedony from Neolithic graves. © Ian Cameron*

Colour plate 18. *Amethyst Crystals. © Ian Cameron*

CHAPTER 5.

Byronic beauty

Pannanich Hill

We used to explore both banks of the river Dee; over the bridge and down Pannanich Road was a regular trek for us. The usual attraction was the remains of the Newfoundlanders' log cabin camp in the woods, quite derelict now, with unlocked doors swinging eerily in the wind.

Today, we will range farther afield. On the banks of the Dee, a short distance east of Ballater Bridge: are ruins on what was once the site of Pannanich Lodge.

Built originally as an inn on the old South Deeside road at the Dalmuchie ferry, it expanded to accommodate the patrons of the mineral waters found on the hill above. There are scant traces of that lodge today, but the sheltering oak, beech and sycamore trees are still there marking the ruins.

Site of Pannanich Lodge. © Ian Cameron

In that, then ostentatious, hostelry the view from the bay windows, of the River Dee, the magnificent backdrop of the Coyles of Muick, and, beyond and above, the towering skyline of Dark Lochnagar must have been inspiring, and certainly proved so to the young Lord Byron.

Imagine for a moment that we are back in 1772; Pannanich Lodge is a bustling place this spring morning, the inn has stabling for the guests' horses and byres and outhouses for its farm. The ferryman is setting out across the Dee to meet the Laird, Francis Farquharson, who he can see approaching on his white mare. The first Ballater Bridge with its five elegant arches is still eleven years off and only ferries on the Dee at Dalmuchie and the ford at Garranmhor serve the early Ballater.

Today Francis Farquharson is off to inspect the progress at the great march dyke he is building east of the mineral wells up on the hill. His work in setting up bathhouses and pumps at the wells was so successful that he has extended Pannanich Lodge to cater for the patrons.

A victim of his own success, Francis was forced to purchase the whole of Pannanich Hill to secure his investment in the mineral wells. He then planted the hill with Scots pine seedlings from his own tree nursery in the field below Monaltrie House.

Look carefully at the fenced area to the right of the straggling row of trees in front of the house: this was the site of Joseph Farquharson's tree nursery from 1772, still visible in this image from 1866. The little pines that first planted out Pannanich hill were grown here.

Joseph Farquharson's nursery also grew the deciduous trees that can still be seen all around us. The great chestnuts trees amidst the houses of Morven Way were originally planted on Monaltrie House's east drive, more of the Laird's chestnuts trees can yet be found at Birkhall House. In the 1700's then known as Sterin House and no doubt a welcome destination of our Joseph Farquharson who lodged nearby at the Manse of Invermuick until Monaltrie house was ready in 1782. Invermuick Manse still boasts a Joseph Farquharson chestnut tree.

The 'Plantation' of trees at Ballater bridge that today forms the 'Keep Left' are five of Joseph Farquharson's chestnut trees, much to small Ballater boys' delight each conker season.

It is worthwhile adding that beech trees were also grown in the Monaltrie nursery; examples of which can be seen lining the brae on the Pass of Ballater beside the 'Fog House', Joseph Farquharson's folly. More beech trees from this prolific source can be seen bordering the South Deeside Road on the way to our Laird's great work at the Pannanich Wells. Just above the actual wells are beech trees dating from this historic time!

Just past the ruins, on a bend of the river is the Craws' Widdie: this is a delightful wood of old Scots Pine, resplendent with deep green needles and orange-barked upper branches that had been home to crows since the ice went away, and each spring was a magnet to young Ballater boys in pursuit of the crows' eggs.

The Dalmuchie burn reaches the Dee at this point, and only a few yards up the burn you could still find the sawdust from an early sawmill that had been driven by water power from a dam farther up the burn in the woods. This sawmill cut Francis Farquharson's 1770s' pine trees, in the mid 1800's, before the ground passed to the McKenzies of Glen Muick.

The McKenzies replanted Pannanich Hill, harvesting the pines in the early 1900s. By the time of the Great War the hill had been replanted again and this third crop was the trees that the men of the Newfoundland Overseas Forestry Unit clear felled in the 1940's to provide pit props for the coal industry in a war-time Britain.

At this point, we return to the road. Only a hundred yards away, a large twin oak tree grows out of the pavement; this is the Wishing Tree, under which generations of young Ballater courting couples have silently embraced while 'wishing'.

Trees for pit props being loaded on Pannanich brae (1942). © Ian Cameron

The Twin Oak Wishing Tree. © Ian Cameron

Pannanich Wells Hotel. © Ian Cameron

We now start to climb Pannanich Brae: on our left a gate is locked across the old South Deeside road. That right of way regains the 'high road' at Glascorrie road end, a half-mile east and is a delightful walk crossing the site of the old Pannanich Hotel golf course (*See colour plate 13*).

Let us carry on the main road today; round the next corner is evidence of the old Pannanich brae granite quarry. That was the scene of a tragic traffic accident in 1941, when two Newfoundlanders were killed. The lumberjacks were buried across the river in Tullich kirkyard.

Pannanich Wells Hotel, right at the top of the hill, was built out of this quarry. This section of road was built specifically to allow easier access to the mineral springs after the first Ballater Bridge was opened in 1783.

Pannanich Lodge and the Dalmuchie ferry fell into decline after Ballater Bridge and Pannanich Wells Hotel were built but the sudden collapse of Ballater Bridge in 1799 gave both a new lease of life until Telford built the second bridge some years later.

Castle Plant extended the little car park at Pannanich Hotel in the 1980s'; at the time I was quite amazed to find slate among the granite that we were excavating. The whole hill is a geologist's dream. The Ballater granite comes into contact here with much older rocks and, as is usual on contact zones, throws out mineral deposits. Hence the Pannanich Mineral Wells of today.

We continue along a couple of hundred yards till we come to the end of the Forestry Commission's ground. Here a massive drystone dyke, a mother of all dykes, marches up the Hill. This is the remaining evidence of our Francis Farquharson's work

The dyke, built in 1772, marks the boundary between the Earl of Aboyne's ground to the east and the recent acquisition of Francis Farquharson's on the west.

We follow the great dyke up the hill; only in its immediate presence, and seeing the enormous foundation stones, can one truly appreciate the superhuman effort that had created it. Talk about the Great Wall of China: we have its equal right here!

Quite close to the dyke, on the GlenTanar side, is a little tree-covered knoll that has puzzled me for many years. There is no heather to be seen, only large boulders and shallow pits. I used to think it prehistoric; the earthworks were old, but somehow it followed no known pattern.

The March Dyke. © Ian Cameron

On my last visit, I realised what it was; this was a 1772 borrow pit for the monster stones that founded the dyke. That brought images of an army of workmen digging out the stones, loading them on sledges, and Highland ponies pulling the loads across to the work at the wall. Again it all came alive; the clues are all around us, we only have to do the interpretation (*See colour plate 14*).

About 150 feet up the hill, the dyke swings to the right; several hundred yards farther on, and 500 feet higher up, we are above the Crags of Pannanich and close by the source of the Dalmuchie burn. There is a lochan here, and running due north is a massive shelf of rock, not granite, but quartzite. The outcrop is faulted and fractured; we could see that the cracks were coated with tiny, intensely red-coloured crystals. In nature, be it mushrooms or crystals, the colour red indicate danger. We took neither chances nor samples, but we did theorise on what we had just seen as we carried on our way.

From our lofty perch, we take a compass reading and strike out to the south-east. That leads us over the ridge of Pannanich Hill; on the skyline, stop and take time to note how this ridge runs north-east till it reaches the River Dee. On the north bank of the Dee, beyond Cambus O'May Bridge, the ridge is re-established as it forms the foothills that run up into Culblean Hill.

At that point, but several thousands of years earlier, the ridge had continued at high level across the current site of the bridge, blocking the drainage of the valley, resulting in a great build-up of water that flooded back into the ice. Torrents erupted along the side of the valley as the trapped water sought to escape out to the lower ground.

Evidence used to be seen on the hillside just above the Cambus quarries as lines running parallel to and above the old workings, but recent tree growth now hides the feature and we have to seek for it in old photographs.

In this old image, the parallel lines above the quarry workings clearly indicate the shore line and the great depth of water impounded behind the obstruction across the valley at the present day site of the Cambus O'May suspension bridge.

Let us continue on our march, south-east. We descend to the Pollagach Burn, which drains the Pollagach Moss and drops down to join the Dee at Inchmarnoch.

The Pollagach Moss was where the Ballater folk held rights to dig peats; they accessed the moss from a hill road west of Braichley House that continued on beyond the peat banks to round the shoulder of Mount Keen and carry on to Glen Mark. That was one of the hill passes that young Deesiders used when they went over to Angus to work at the harvest, before returning to their own late crop. It was also a route for the Morven-stilled whisky on its way to a thirsty Dundee.

Cambus O'May quarries. © Ian Cameron

Perched on the hillside across the burn is the Rocking Stone; this erratic, at some time long past, was deposited by retreating ice on a bed of boulders. By merest chance, the stone is so well-balanced that it could be made to rock gently on its base by hand pressure.

The phenomenon was not lost on the old people, and we find this stone incorporated in their ley-line mythology.

When I started on this book, I promised myself, and others, that I would write solely on my knowledge of Deeside minerals. I knew then that I was kidding myself, but it is only as I write, that the facts, the stories, and my new discoveries come rushing to mind and I know that to tell the full story of the minerals, I must include the myths.

I digress, but nearly seven miles away, on a compass reading of 279 degrees, lies the site of an ancient chapel at Rinabaich, just north of the busy A93. There is one remaining standing stone, and, as we have seen, the early church simply annexed these pagan sites.

There is very little to be seen at Rinabaich; it lies very close to the A93, there is a very recent cairn above the site and a standing stone on the level below. There is little doubt that this is a prehistoric site that long predated the recorded Christian chapel dedicated to St.Manire.

Rinabaich. © Ian Cameron

Most prehistoric sites on Deeside have suffered from destruction from invaders, and the usual suspects were the Danes, according to the old writers. Be that as it may, there is evidence at Rinabaich that the original structure had been destroyed in the search for treasure.

The remaining standing stone is mistakenly called a pulpit stone; this name comes from the lectern-like top of the stone. In fact, the stone has been interfered with at some point in its history and is actually re-erected upside down!

If you study the construction of stone circles, you will find that the ancients often selected, or indeed shaped, the foot of their stones, like the one at Rinabaich, to allow easier socketing in a hole in the ground. Study the drawing below.

How it was done.

On a straight line from Rinabaich to our Rocking Stone, this 'ley-line' crosses the River Dee. At the exact point where the 'line' meets the south bank of the River Dee, there is a wide vein of quartz: this vein reputedly carries silver.

Our 'line' now joins the B976 and follows it to Girnoc Bridge, and on till it reaches Strath Girnoc Farm road end: at this point our 'line' carries straight on through the woods of the Knock Hill and reappears at the Knock Castle. See 'Plant and Roots'

As I have indicated before, 16th.Century castles would certainly have occupied older, much earlier sites.

The 'line' now passes close to the Druids' stone at Dallyfour, and regains the line of the B976 road before crossing the River Muick at the old Kirk.

This section of our 'ley line' has recently been greatly enhanced with the planting of deciduous trees, which will in time give a pleasing avenue effect. I like to think that the ancients would have approved.

The Knock Castle. © Ian Cameron

Here again at the Bridge of Muick, the old Christian church would have annexed an earlier pagan site.

The 'line' now heads straight up over the summit of Pannanich Hill to arrive neatly at the Rocking Stone!

The whole glen from here down to Ballaterach Farm is a Site of Special Scientific Interest, teeming with unusual geology; there is a similarity here to the situation up Glengairn, but here it is the GlenTanar limestone that is coming into contact with the granite. The minerals recorded here are wollastonite, tremolite and garnets, all skarn minerals found on the perimeter of the granite aureole.

The ley line at Dallyfour straight and the Druid's stone. © Ian Cameron

The Pollagach gap, as it is known, is prone to violent rain storms that in a short space of time turn the burn into a very dangerous raging torrent. In the summer of 1950, I can remember, a cloud burst happening above Creag an t-Seabhaig in the Pass of Ballater. The mass of water was so great that it tore a great gouge on the hillside, creating a raging burn where there had never been a burn before. A whole section of the wood disappeared and raw rock and gravel were left exposed for years. The strange thing was that the cloudburst happened directly over the most highly mineralised area of the hill that hosted the lead.

In my Forestry Commission days, we lived at Dunkeld; John Corbett, the head forester who had planted Allt Cailleach forest above Birkhall House, finished his career at Craigvinean forest at Dunkeld. He would sit in his house and watch severe electrical storms rage over Craigvinean Hill followed by torrential rain.

John always declared that it was the minerals in the hill that attracted the lightning. It would seem to me that the minerals in the Pollagach Gap act in the same way.

Ballaterach was where the young Lord Byron and his mother stayed when convalescing and taking the waters at Pannanich Wells. He apparently was a most unruly child, totally out of control, who delighted in creating havoc with the locals' animals and belongings. They, of course, could not retaliate.

The local mill-wright, an Isaac Calder of Greystones, had an absolute terror of the boy coming into his workshop, equipped as it was with dangerous unguarded machinery; he simply shut up shop when he saw the young Byron appear.

Quite co-incidentally, but still relevantly to our tale, that Isaac Calder's daughter, Margaret, married a Charles Stewart who was killed by lightning in the Pollagach Gap on 8th August 1849. Charles Stewart was an excise man and doubtless died in the line of duty.

The Pollagach Moss, like the Braes of Morven, harboured the whisky stills and the wild men that ran them.

On Deeside, the most violent electrical storms always seem to occur in the month of August.

Up on the hill above Ballaterach Farm stands Ettrick Croft. An old couple used to live there. They had accumulated many interesting stones, arrow heads and crystals and I had been invited to visit.

Hill people tend to cart home anything strange they find on their land, and that certainly proved to be the case here. Outside the door there were white quartz stones and many fragments of red chalcedony; a shapeless, heavy mass of grey material caught my eye, Jimmy just said that he had 'picked it up'. I later identified it as hydrozincite, a not-at-all common mineral.

In the house, they had a collection of flint arrowheads, more chalcedony and carnelian fragments, and the most perfect cairngorms crystal that I have ever seen. Bella told me that her father had brought it home from his work at the Cambus o' May quarries.

Jimmy with one of his curios. © Ian Cameron

While doing research on Neolithic times; I discovered that that same chalcedony, so abundant in the Ettrick fields was often found in graves all over the North-east, and had been dated back 4000 years. The flint arrowheads had also been found locally, all indicators of a busy past at Ettrick (*See colour plate 17*).

The way back to Ballater was simply by the South Deeside road from Inchmarnoch Bridge, or alternatively, through the Cambus o' May woods to the suspension bridge at the old Cambus station.

In my early memories, that wood was a truly mythical 'Wood of Caledon' like place such as our conservationists' dream of recreating. The trees were a mixture of mature oaks and magnificent old pines. In spring, the ground was covered with cowslips, primroses, wood anemones, bluebells and anthills, and, later in the year, mushrooms.

All that changed one Saturday morning, 31st January 1953; (see 'Plant and Roots') a hurricane-force east wind uprooted most of the trees. Few remain, and the wood was replanted, mostly with Sitka spruce, dark, dense and alien.

CHAPTER 6.

Granite meets Gabbro

Morven Hill

The name Morven can be interpreted as the Hill of the Great Divide; this divide is most evident where the Coinlach burn cuts deeply into the hill, taking advantage of the weak rock structures at the contact between the granite of Culblean and the gabbros of Morven (*See colour plate 15*).

The rock exposures in the bed of the Coinlach burn were one of Dr Heddle's amethysts locations. He also deduced that their distinctive purple colour came from contact with ferric acids and manganese minerals. Time has proved him correct in those assumptions.

The contact between granite and gabbro is more evident with snow cover. © Ian Cameron

Time moved on to the Iron Age; Deeside and its granite were short of the iron-ores now sought. Not so to the east of Morven: here the whole Balronald face is rich in iron-stone. This is the source of Dr Heddle's ferric acid that coloured the Coinlach burn amethysts; it is also the source of the Irie Well mineral spring on the ridge above Balronald face (*See colour plate 18*).

The Bristol Blenheim Mk IV. © Ian Cameron

During the war, on the 19th October 1943, a RAF Bristol Blenheim bomber flew into the side of Morven in fog, the tragedy caused; it was said, by a compass deceived by the great mass of iron in the hill.

That aircraft, T1863 from Inverness, failed to clear the 2861ft- high Morven by 400 feet. The wreckage was buried at the crash site but, only now, sections are emerging from the peat. There were no reported survivors.

Crash site on Morven. © Ian Cameron

The Iron Age folk built a fort high on Morven, overlooking and guarding their homes in their settlements of Devonha around the Lochs of Davan and Kinord of today.

The Iron Age hill forts are often termed 'vitrified'. That description intrigued me. I learnt that it had been found that certain hill forts contained, in the ruins of their walls, residues and fragments of evidence that the walls had been burnt, and fused together.

In my research I found that only hills composed of ironstone, or 'blue stone' as they were called after the colour of a freshly broken stone, were capable of vitrification. The hill forts walls were constructed from the rocks at hand on top of the hill, and, as we have seen elsewhere, limestone is often found in association with the ironstone. The two rocks types would have been used to build a wall that was interlaced with heavy wooden logs to form a palisade against attack.

In normal circumstances, that was a secure defensive position, but when put to the ultimate test and set on fire, it became a trap. Built as they were on the top of hills, once the timber caught light in the uphill draught the fort's walls were subjected to tremendous heat. Heat so intense that the ironstone started to smelt, the limestone acted as a flux speeding the reaction and creating the glassy slag that gives the remains its 'vitrified' name today.

For myself, I made another discovery. In my Forestry Commission days, much of the work was repair-welding ploughs and tractors that had failed on the rough ground. The introduction of low-hydrogen type welding rods with their stronger welding properties greatly simplified my task. Those rods were characterised by leaving an amber-coloured slag on the weld.

Imagine my astonishment and wonder on seeing that same amber 'vitrified' slag on 2000 year-old walls at Dunnideer, Tap of Noth and Morven!

The whole Howe of Cromar thrived in the Iron Age with its own source of ironstone to fuel its culture and good fertile clay ground for its new farmers. Iron smelting hearths are still being found, hill forts abound on Mullachdhu, Upper Ruthven, and Cairnmore. The Blue Cairn, a huge cairn surrounded by a stone circle, sadly under-rated, lies neglected and hidden in the new plantations above Balgrennie.

Iron Age hill fort on Morven. © Ian Cameron

The evidence of the Picts' time in the Howe can be seen in the numerous place-names starting with Pit: Pitline, Pitellachie, Pitentaggart among many others; additionally, there is a wealth of Pictish art carved in their standing stones.

One source of their iron came from the eskers or sand deposits that litter the 'Howe o' Cromar'. The sand was water washed into the once great post glacial lake that today has its fossil remains in Loch Kinord and Davan. The sands compose of the glacial ground down debris from the surrounding hills, and where the origin rock was iron stone; there you find the black sands. When Iron Age man made this discovery he set up his hearths. The black sands were the source of his purest iron (*See colour plate 20*).

The most enduring, and to me fascinating, discovery of this howe is the long relationship between the early iron smelting hearths and the last smiddy left at Smiddyhill; there has been continuous iron working here for more than 2000 years!

Half way through this time period: in the days of the early King James's of Scotland, and here I quote from John Grant's 'Legends of The Braes O' Mar'

'Near the Castle of Migvie is the farm of Smiddiehill, and, though now united to the lands of Migvie, it was in the old days a lairdship by itself. It became so in a singular manner.

The king, whichever king it was, was hotly pursued by some offended tribe, and, as they were more nimble of foot, with difficulty he made the nearest house, that of Smiddiehill, then occupied by a smith, or gow, of the name of Reid.

The Gow, finding his sovereign's life in such jeopardy, and the house being incapable of defence, fell upon the following stratagem to cheat the enemy of their prey.

He resembled the king much in person, and, having exchanged clothes with him, sallied boldly forth, and, running full against the nearest foe, felled him to the earth, and fled away at full speed. All the others, as the smith expected, made sure he was the king, and pursued him with ravenous appetite for his blood. The race was not long, brave Gow.

He was overtaken and slain at a small streamlet about a mile from Smiddiehill on the Strathdon road. The place is still called Strath-gow.

While the loyal smith lost his life, the king saved his. In gratitude he gave to the widow as much land as she could run over — under certain most distressing conditions — the which the curious antiquary may learn from the natives of the place. She girt up her loins, and ran over nine rich acres, and at last sunk exhausted where it is called Killy-groan. Thus the Reids came to reign at Smiddyhill.'

This most mediaeval of land measurement methods reminded me of the ancient Spanish unit of measurement, cabellerias - denoting the area a horse could be ridden round at a brisk walking pace in one hour.

CHAPTER 7.

Quarry questing

The Cambus Quarries

One of our little friends lived in a house at Cambus o' May. One Monday, he came to school in a great excitement: he had gone up to the quarries that weekend and had seen wonderful things. We must all have an expedition there next Saturday.

Saturday came, a fine day, and three of us biked to the Cambus quarries. The quarry road was no longer used, but it had been well made and had carried Ballater's granite building stone by horse and cart, traction engine and motor truck from the early 1800s till the late 1940s.

As we approached the actual quarry, we could see that it consisted of many individual quarries on the hillside at all different levels. When you entered any particular level, the great scale of the workings struck you: the granite was cut clean up to 80 feet. The quarry floor then was still littered with cranes, winches and air pipe, but high above us noisy ravens and silent hawks had found the most ideal nesting places.

Turning around, the view of the Dee valley ranged from Lochnagar, looking nearer than usual, to Pannanich Hotel perched on its hill across the river, with, in the foreground, the mid-day train panting up the track to Ballater, a banner of smoke marking its progress.

The cranes used, and indeed developed in the North East of Scotland granite quarries, were of the Scotch derrick design; cranes that were built mainly by Henderson the Engineers in King Street, Aberdeen.

Originally manually operated, they were first provided with steam power, then, as the cranes appeared in civil engineering work everywhere from hydro-electric dams to the very top of the towers of the Forth Road Bridge, electricity became the power of choice.

The last crane. © Ian Cameron

The Royal Bridge. © Ian Cameron

Although ultimately developed as a civil engineering tool, this crane was actually invented by one Thomas Derrick, an Elizabethan hangman, who built his device to help mass produce his 3000 executions at Tyburn, London.

Two derrick cranes, one steam, the other manual are shown in a Washington Wilson photo of the construction of Ballater Bridge in the 1880s.

We found the remains of the blacksmith's shop still complete in those days with its bellows and forge. Many years later, my friend, Charlie Clark, the Bridge of Gairn blacksmith, told me: that when he came to leave school his three elder brothers were already working in his father's smiddy with the result that and he was sent to serve his apprenticeship at the Cambus quarry. There he learnt how to sharpen and temper the stone-masons' tools. He went on to explain this skill. First the blunt tools had to be heated in the forge and left to cool slowly in order to remove all hardness. The tools were heated up again and shaped and sharpened by hammer blows on the anvil. The final heating was followed by rubbing the sharpened edge on the smiddy floor to reveal 'the temper colours'. On the bright steel the colours could be seen moving slowly down the tool to the cutting edge. The art was to arrest the desired colour the correct distance from the tip by placing the tool upright in a wooden box containing a small amount of water.

I asked Charlie how he knew when everything was just right.

"Quite simple" said he. "You wait till the temper colour is straw, then when it is the length of an ear of corn from the tip of the tool you quench it in that water box."

As easy as that, yet a skill that few mastered or retained. Interesting though to see how Charles used agricultural terms of colour and dimensions: no metrics or inches, just the length of an ear of corn. Charlie learnt his trade in these quarries before the First World War, and when I knew him in the 1970's he was the only blacksmith on Deeside left with that skill.

Just beyond the smiddy was a very solid magazine that had held the black gunpowder, and I can remember the mortar and pestle that were used to prepare the charges still being there

We examined the quarries individually, our friend keeping his secrets till last. It so happened that the quarry nearest Ballater was the special one; as you entered there was an almost complete crane attached to massive granite blocks. The rails that had carried the stones on bogies were still there: you could trace where the bogies had dumped the discarded cuttings over the tip. It was all so real: the quarriers had built a substantial bothie against the quarry wall: it did not take a lot of imagination to visualise the last act here, as the players had left all their props behind.

But the best was still to come. What had really excited our little friend was the right-hand wall of this quarry. The ground around us was reverting to the heather that the quarriers had stripped away, and young firs and birches were reclaiming their hill. That wall, however, had a mineral vein running vertically through it, sandwiched between the great granite blocks in a similar fashion to the ones in the Pass of Ballater. That vein was neither lead-nor tungsten-bearing, but I recognised fluorspar, except it was not green, as at Abergairn, but an azure/violet colour. We were well acquainted with fluorine from Abergairn: that was the mineral we ground down, sprinkled on a coal shovel and heated on the fire. At a quite low temperature, the powder would issue brilliant coloured sparks that jumped off the shovel, just like fireworks. The real surprise was the main constituent of that vein; it was a scaly, pink material that I had never seen before, it was heavy, very, very heavy, but quite soft and we could break it down to a powder easily.

We trailed samples home, and even the chemistry teacher could not tell us what it was. Some sort of 'spar' we were told; just as well there was no 'open all hours' shop chain then or we really would have been confused.

The mystery mineral was barium sulphate, or barytes to the mining fraternity, or barite to our North American friends.

Barytes is used as the barium meal in medicine, it is used to give golf balls their weight, it is added to rubber in tyres, it is used in paint, it is used to caulk boats and most importantly, barytes is the main constituent of 'drilling mud'. And, by the 1970s, with North Sea oil getting into its stride, barytes was suddenly one very sought after commodity (*See colour plate 19*).

CHAPTER 8.

Garnets on the Gairn

Glengairn is, geologically, a very complex mix that is still being unravelled, and in so being is revealing ever more great truths. Those truths, at the back of your mind, you felt you should have known all the time: they made you stop and think: 'Why didn't I work that out?'

The evidence is all around us. The old people hinted at the truths with their Gaelic place names, the great veins intercepting on top of Carn Dearg, the 'Red Hill', the massive exposure of limestone that is the Mammie Hill, the 'Ringing Stone' at Richarkarie; all we had to do was sit down and look.

Dr Heddle knew the short cut to mineral knowledge; it was to examine freshly exposed bedrock. Glen Gairn in the 19th.Century was a geologist's dream. The Improvements had been slow in coming to upper Gairnside, and then lime quarries were opened up on both sides of the glen. It was there and then Dr.Heddle came to visit (*See colour plate 21*).

By far the greatest limestone workings were on Dalnabo Hill. Today, Dalnabo Hill is a delightful open lime-loving juniper, larch and birch wood: in Heddle's time it would have been bare, grazed down mostly by goats. Here I must digress; the last haulage track on Dalnabo Hill, from the Glen Gairn road up to the lime quarry, forms a splendid walk (*See colour plate 23*).

The old tracks in Glen Gairn, and indeed all over the Cairngorms area, contrast sharply with the more recent Land Rover tracks that scar the mountains.

The old tracks were built to the criterion of creating a constant gradient that a horse could comfortably climb, and as such, they adapt to the contours of the hills and neither offends the eye nor do they allow run-off water to reach the critical speed of erosion.

The war-surplus Jeeps, and later Land Rovers, came on the hill after the war; they indeed made possible the new concept of commercial game sport. The track-building criteria changed drastically; the gradients were limited only by the Jeep's cross-country capabilities, and, to save time and money, the gamekeeper's instructions to the bull-dozer driver were simple: make the road to the butts by the shortest possible route. The result is the scars we see today.

Back to Dalnabo Larch Wood.

Where did the larch come from? Just upstream, Major Caulfield's 1751 military bridge crosses the Gairn. Larch trees from Atholl were planted there to help stabilize the earthworks on the northern abutment; these were amongst the first European Larch ever seen in Aberdeenshire. Over time, those trees seeded and spread downwind in a new larch wood that soon crossed the River Gairn and colonized Dalnabo Hill. A natural forest.

Each autumn, this Dalnabo larch wood continues to send armadas of seeds downstream. Floating off on the waters of the Gairn to colonize riverbanks, extravagantly so, at the mouth of the Gairn where it meets the River Dee. From that point east larch trees of Dalnabo origin can be found growing on each bank of the river, where they create their own larch wood satellite colonies all the way to the sea.

This illustrates the case for the moving forest. In this instance, transport by wind and water. The Forest of Caledon so beloved by conservationists was never wall to wall forestation. Wind, water, fire, animals, man and indeed altitude all played their parts in restricting, and constantly redrawing its footprint.

The most ancient trees on the hill are around 140 years old; indicating that they had crossed the Gairn about 1866: by that time the lime quarry's busiest days would have been over.

A study of the ground, tracks, and excavations shows that many smaller trials for lime had been made before settling on the main quarry. Heddle found red garnets, a complete series of lime-rich garnets, wollastonite, dark green grossular, diopside and the jade-like idocrase in the quarry. The presence of those minerals has caused the site, in recent years, to be declared a Site of Special Scientific Interest.

Limestone, like quartz, has always held a fascination for me. In my Forestry Commission days I often stopped on my way to Loch Rannoch for a tea-break at an old lime quarry on the shoulder of Schiehallion Mountain. This was during my mad mineral phase, and I used to search for crystals in the rocks there. Imagine my surprise one day to find perfectly preserved fossil sea shells, almost two thousand feet above sea level!

I have revisited that location many times since that day in 1964, but I could never again find this source of wonder and I began to think that I had imagined it.

Fast forward to June this year when an enforced extended holiday in Madeira saw me with time to visit 'Rota da Cal,' translated, 'the lime route,' on the north of the island. Here again my curiosity got the better of me! How could there be a limestone on a volcanic island? Just inland from St.Vincente on the north coast of Madeira lay the source of my quest; on a blisteringly hot afternoon the tour bus dropped me off in the midst of a leafy laurel and beech forest at the top of a steep track. Presently two youths appeared and we climbed up to the first of two lime quarries. The quarries were mere caves in the rock, more in the fashion of mines; here the islanders had been extracting limestone since the 17th.Century.

I learnt that this natural resource had been exploited until the 1960's. Indeed my young guide was the grandson of the last lime worker. The lime route was the tortuous path the workers had taken with 60kg loads on their backs to the limekiln where the limestone was loaded between layers of dry wood, and latterly mineral coal as it became available with Madeira's growing importance as a coaling station for steamers. The kiln would then be set alight to reduce the limestone (calcium carbonate) to burned lime (calcium oxide).

The kiln could burn for several days to achieve the 900 degrees C. required for the reaction, and then take another few days to cool. The end product was used to improve agricultural land, and in Madeira, with a particularly pure product, it was also used in paint and masonry work. But the question remained: how did the limestone come to be here in a volcanic island? 20 Million years ago there was an underwater eruption on the Atlantic seabed. Over time successive eruptions spewed out lava until the volcanic mass rose above the surface of the water and created a new island. Today Madeira is an island perched on the top of a mountain that rises 5000 metres from the floor of the ocean.

Great slabs of the sea floor were lifted thousands of feet by volcanic activity and frozen within the solidifying lava hundreds of feet above the Atlantic Ocean, in the new formed land. These sections of seabed were already limestone, full of fossilised sea urchins, bivalves, shells and coral, before the uplift.

The inquisitive individual who first found the limestone high on the hills inland from St.Vincente is not recorded; but this source was worked continuously until only 50 years ago.

Scallop shell fossilised in Rota da Cal limestone. © Ian Cameron

My young guide showed me fossil specimens of shells recovered from the limestone deposit, which I immediately related to the specimens I had seen on Schiehallion so long ago.

Everything came into perspective; the uplifting of sea floor had happened in Scotland too, only many, many millions of years earlier than this much more recent event that I was now deciphering. I was in good company, for when I returned to Scotland and Abergairn, I read a review of Rebecca Stott's new book: 'Darwin's Ghosts.' In this excellent book she tells of Leonardo da Vinci's similar wonder as he ponders the oyster shell fossils he finds embedded in rocks high on the Tuscan hills!

As you walk into the old graveyard at the Fit o'Gairn just beneath our house at Abergairn, the first thing you notice is how the rows of gravestones all face east and to the Holy Land. The long-ruined chapel in their midst is similarly orientated. The old folk had an empathy with nature and the metaphysical that their pre-Reformation Faith had nurtured with imagery and grace that endures to keep this a special place still.

Amongst the older graves is that of Father Lachlan McIntosh, the Catholic Priest, who lived at Ardoch above Dalfad. Indeed Glengairn, along with the Braes of Mar and Glenlivet, supported enclaves of Roman Catholicism that the Reformers passed by. The McGregors of Dalfad felt sufficiently emboldened, to erect a tall crucifix on the slopes of the Mammie hill to broadcast their persuasion to the world.

Although widely regarded as renegades and cattle thieves, the McGregors were Lairds of Dalfad in their own right; they lived in Glengairn for more than 100 years from 1634 until long after the 1745 rebellion. A staunchly Catholic family, that sent their sons to be priests and teachers, built a chapel in the Dalfad birch woods and farmed extensively at Dalfad, Ardoch and Inverenzie in Gairnside, and also at Auchallater beyond Braemar and Wester Micras in Crathie. All these localities are notable in having both limestone quarries and kilns.

Old records talk of the 'McGregors of the lime', and bearing in mind the agricultural 'improvements' movement of that time, it is interesting to note that the lime-rich Mammie hill would have been part of their Dalfad ground and the evidence of lime quarrying above Ardoch, still to be seen today, would have been a later and perhaps even more legitimate McGregor enterprise. There can be little doubt that the McGregors were the pioneers of lime working in Glen Gairn and Upper Deeside.

Above Dalfad, Dr. Heddle found cinnamon coloured garnets in the Mammie Hill quarries; the limestone here was brought down to be burnt in a large kiln on the old road up to the Ardoch Farm.

My sojourn in Madeira gave me great insight into the extraction and processing of the limestone there in very recent times, but by the same primitive, labour intensive methods that had been used in Glen Gairn by the McGregors and others in the 1700's. This elucidation gave me great affinity with that time and peoples.

I digress here again, but, far from Glen Gairn, over in Glen Buchat there is a celebrated 'garnet stone'. Perched high on a hillside above Smiddyford Farm, that large boulder was attracting 'rock hounds' from far and near. A local contractor got to hear of it, and, craving instant wealth brought a compressor on to the hill. He duly drilled and blasted the garnet stone, succeeding in breaking it in half, and shattering all the remaining garnets in it. The stones had a real red fire, were of gem quality, and some were as large as a 10p coin.

On the same hill are to be found rose quartz, rock crystal and tourmaline. Showing red garnets and sockets of much larger ones.

The Garnet Stone, author and Ben. © Ian Cameron

CHAPTER 9.

Tracing the tin

Gairnshiel

When we cross Gairnshiel Bridge, we enter an area of intense geological interest. The first people that came here after the 'ice went away' were primarily hunter/gatherers, but later became prospectors to source the raw ores to smelt into their Bronze Age metal. There is abundant evidence that they were successful. In the late 1800s, two bronze axe heads were found cached in a crevice of the Pass of Ballater rocks, and along with the bronzes were the Glens of Foundland slate moulds that had cast them. In the River Gairn nearby was discovered one of the only two Bronze Age daggers ever found in Scotland (*See colour plate 24*).

All our Bronze Age man needed were the ingredients, copper, zinc and tin. The zinc ores were found at Abergairn, but where was the tin? I struggled with that for years till it was finally confirmed by the British Geological Survey that along with molybdenite, the tin ores, cassiterite and stannite were present in the diorite/granite outcrop at Gairnshiel.

Gairnshiel with an ancient enclosure on the hill. © Ian Cameron

It never fails to amaze me how knowledge is acquired and accumulated. Over time Castle Plant diggers have uncovered iron-age works and older; we have come to recognise the paved walkways of the ancients. The moment I saw a portion of walkway, stones that had been set up more than three thousand Glengairn winters ago, I knew that their Bronze Age mine was not far away. I discovered the vein and saw how they had quarried the copper ore back into the hill creating a worked-out area that nature had long since taken over. To me this was the site, and very tangible proof, of the early metalliferous activities on Glengairn. To me then the riddle was solved; bronze was cast on Gairnside from local ore (*See colour plate 25*).

The tin ores of stannite and cassiterite are disseminated through the diorite. The molybdenite is found in a vein in the massive outcrop, high on the hill immediately before you as you cross the Military Bridge. That area is bounded to the east by a fault hidden under the Kirkstyle mill dam, and to the north by a point near the 'Ringing Stone' at the roadside above Richarkarie.

The Ringing Stone

The Ringing Stone is actually in two parts, having been split along its length; the ringing portion is lying at right angles to and bearing on the other. The bell-like sounds that can be heard on striking the stone betray its very metallic origin, and its probable high nickel iron ore composition. If a magnet is held to the stone there is strong magnetic attraction.

The Ringing Stone. © Ian Cameron

Immediately besides the ringing stone is a lime kiln, but its' very mass and undoubted weight would have ruled out the stone's having been brought here to burn for lime. The deep striation marks suggest that it is much more probable that it was transported by ice from the metal-rich outcrop nearby just north of the Gairnshiel Bridge.

How did the early prospectors find their minerals?

Obviously they made for the high ground to access rock outcrops; from time to time nature helped with cloudbursts that tore out great quantities of soil and rock, lying bare the minerals below. A wind-blown tree with upended root plate can hold a selection of under-lying stone and rock, indeed a major Argentinean emerald mine was originally discovered in this fashion. Vegetation is scarce above mineral deposits, and a trained eye can spot mineral-tolerant plants.

But historically, going back to the Bible, minerals were found by divination. That could take different forms: the traditional hazel wand used for water divining was also used for minerals, especially silver, while ash was preferred for copper and iron rods were always used to find gold.

Again, in my Forestry Commission days on Loch Rannoch-side, an old crofter saw us draining on the hill above his croft. He came over and asked if we would cut a drain across his very wet field. It was late on Friday afternoon, and we were coming down off the hill anyway, so we agreed to help. First it had to be decided the line of the drain; the old man went across to a fence and twisted off two short lengths of wire: these he bent into L shapes.

He then walked across the field with the wires held out before him; to our great astonishment, the wires suddenly crossed, the crofter marked the spot with a stone, then continued on till he reached the road-side ditch, all the time marking the wires' reaction points with stones. We were then invited to plough along the line of stones, and, sure enough, we found water under each stone and by the time we reached the roadside ditch we had a real burn running. I asked the crofter where he had learned to water-divine, but all he said was 'Anyone can do it.'

Having witnessed that spectacle, I am willing to believe that Bronze Age man would have had similar powers.

After Japan bombed Pearl Harbor on the 7th December 1941, the United States went to war with Japan and Germany. There then swiftly swung into action a concentrated war effort focused on factories' planned output of munitions, tanks, trucks and planes, and shipyards' construction of warships.

All that production depended on ready supplies of iron, copper, aluminium and all other metals; and this in turn depended on the availability of vast tonnages of mineral ores.

The US Government had a new hi-tech method of locating the minerals; they supplied their geologists with ultra-violet lamps. At night, the lamps would pick out the colours given off rocks that were then compared with a chart. This chart indicating the colours that specific minerals emitted when subjected to the ultra-violet light. This instant prospecting aid resulted in great areas of Utah and Arizona being turned into mines very rapidly, providing the minerals needed for the war industries.

Old war time copper mine in Arizona. © Ian Cameron

CHAPTER 10.

Peat for heat

The Fairy Bolt

Bob Shaw (6th from the left) in 1950 picture of Braemar "Heavies" from Braemar Games Book. © Ian Cameron

In 1909, Bob Shaw was born at Inverenzie Farm in Glengairn, at the junction of the Glen Fenzie burn and the Gairn. Bob lived most of his life at Inverenzie, but his great claim to fame was his years competing at Highland Games as a 'Heavies' athlete. Bob's forte was putting the shot, and at that sport he had no equal for many years. Bob was in his prime just before the Second World War and for some years afterwards.

As farmers at Inverenzie, the Shaws would have lived and worked in Glengairn as tenants of the Morven lairds, the Keillers, of Dundee marmalade fame. Their farm year was governed by the seasons, and more often by the weather, high on the Glengairn hills. It was a hard life, a struggle in survival for even keeping themselves fed and warm.

Fire, and the basic need for heat, has always figured in Highland folk lore; in 'Plant and Roots' I tell of the fire rituals nearby at Stranlea. Central to fire has always been the casting, drying and carting home of peat; and the peat moss for Inverenzie fuel was high on Wester Morven.

The casting of peat was done in dry summer weather, as the peat mosses could be wet, boggy places. Peat deposits, like coal seams, varied wildly in quality, but the peat to be won on Wester Morven was renowned for its consistency and good, clean burning properties.

The Shaws attributed that to the sheer depth of peat found there; horses and sledges could negotiate it, but of the later tractor era, there is nothing but horror stories.

Peat was traditionally cut in the warm months of May and June. The wet oblong peats were left to drip on top of the bank, another visit set them up in little stacks to dry and finally, when deemed ready for the fire, they were barrowed out to the track to be carted home. The whole process was labour-intensive and time-consuming and could take up the best part of a month. Neighbours would band together to see the winter fuel secured as a community activity, similar to the sheep gathering, clipping and dipping. As with the lime, and, incidentally, the lime kilns used great quantities of peat, the peat mosses on Upper Deeside and Glen Gairn went into decline with the advent of the railway and the arrival of cheap coal at Ballater.But in the glens limited peat cutting survived; partly because the peat was free, other than the labour, and partly because of tradition.

As a young man in the late 1920s, Bob Shaw was one of a party that went to the moss on Wester Morven. They started the casting and lifting the wet peats, and then the rain came on and sent them home for that day. Next day Bob returned to the moss, and found, bright and shiny from the rain, a flint arrowhead. I had the privilege recently of taking this photo of the arrowhead, resting in the jewellery case that has been its home for the past 70 years (*See colour plate 26*).

The fifty pence coin gives scale to the photo; the arrowhead is of early Neolithic age, and as such predates our Bronze Age. Without the aid of carbon dating, I reckon that the late Bob Shaw's arrowhead is at least 5000 years old.

The manufacture of flint artefacts was a skill all of its own. You can note the fretted, serrated edges of the flint; the fracture of flint is known as conchoidal, which means simply: that when chipped the broken surface takes on a semi-circular edge. The art of shaping flint arrowheads takes advantage of that type of fracture.

Archaeologists have given the manufacture a name: knapping, after the technique employed.

Thirty miles down the Dee valley from Morven, on the south bank of the river, is a place called Knappach. That is where a quantity of pigmy flints was found in 1905; in the following years up to 1912 other localities with flint were found around Banchory on both banks of the Dee. The pigmy flints were smaller and much older than Bob Shaw's arrowhead, rarely being more than a half-inch long, but certainly of Stone Age, 5000 to 4000 BC.

I have included the arrowhead, like the Pass of Ballater bronze axes, to authenticate the existence of both Bronze and Stone Age peoples in our glens.

For elaborating on the peat bogs, I offer no apology. Firstly, peat is itself defined as a rock, and so fits neatly within my remit, and secondly: the work at the peat mosses figures, again and again, in our culture. In 'Plant and Roots' the slaughter of the seven Gordon sons is staged :-'On the peat moss.'

Again we can only guess at how this exquisite object came to be found in the Moss at Morven. Did it come on a hunting trip? Or was it war? The arrowhead was found at an altitude of 1400 feet, well above the flooded valleys and yet only a couple of hundred feet above the local settlement level for hut circles.

Peat has the propensity to preserve; in my Forestry Commission days on Rannoch Moor, the draining ploughs were continually hauling centuries-old pine trees out of the bog. Those trees were so fresh that you could smell the rossit (resin); the workers used to cut kindling from them to light their bothie fires, yet six months out of the peat and the great trees had turned to dust. In the case of the arrowhead, Bob Shaw left no indication of there being any other remains found with it.

The Morven hill our arrowhead's original owner knew would not have been very different from the one of today; but there would not have been roads, fences, gates or padlocks. The only man-made objects on the hill would have been clearance cairns and hut circles. The wildlife would have been more obvious; wolves and wild boar still had centuries to roam the hills, and Morven would have had its historic three pairs of golden eagles nesting. One pair would be on the Eagles' nest at the blue rock, high on the east side of Morven; another pair at Castle Wilson in the Slacks of Glencarvie, and a third at the head of Glen Beg. All were soaring in the Morven thermals in living memory, but, sadly, no more.

Colour plate 19. *Barytes.* © *Ian Cameron*

Colour plate 20. *Iron Age man's purest iron.* © *Ian Cameron*

Colour plate 21. *Garnetiferous fragment in quartz breccias.* © Ian Cameron

Colour plate 22. *Garnets in Limestone.* © Ian Cameron

Colour plate 23. *Dalnabo Larch Wood. © Ian Cameron*

Colour plate 24. *Pass of Ballater Bronze Axe heads. © Ian Cameron*

Colour plate 25. *Molybdenite in quartz.* © *Ian Cameron*

Colour plate 26. *The Morven Flint Arrow Head* © *Ian Cameron with kind permission of the late Bob Shaw jnr.*

Colour plate 27. *Corrybeg Stone Circle.* © *Ian Cameron*

Colour plate 28. *The Dee Valley as under water.* © *Ian Cameron*

Colour plate 29. *Sunset on Lochnagar on the Shortest Day as seen from the Corrybeg Circle.* © *Ian Cameron*

Colour plate 30. *Replacing the Flanking stones. © Ian Cameron*

Colour plate 31. *The mineral vein on Carn Dearg. © Ian Cameron*

Colour plate 32. *The vein material.* © Ian Cameron

Colour plate 33. *The soup of minerals.* © Ian Cameron

Colour plate 34. *Quartz breccia. © Ian Cameron*

Colour plate 35. *The quartz with beryl. © Ian Cameron*

Colour plate 36. *Corrie at the Slate Quarry on Meall Dubh. © Ian Cameron*

CHAPTER 11.

Keepers finders

Blue Cairngorms

Around 80 years ago, a game-keeper lived in the lodge at Loch Builg. Stories are told of his gem-hunting skills. Apparently he discovered a source of blue stones: they have been described as 'blue cairngorms', but at that time all crystals found in the hills were called 'cairngorms'.

The keeper apparently traded his blue gems for provisions at the Crathie post office, with the postmaster sending the surplus stones away to a jeweller for sale. That part is certainly true; I have been in the company of the third generation of the postmaster's family - when the stones were being discussed.

The old keeper never disclosed the source of his gems - all rock hounds know the story - and the Loch Builg area has been searched for the last 70 summers, but to no reported avail.

The post master's family did have some of the stones mounted as jewellery; but all that remain today is a pair of earrings only one of which is original. In the mineral hunters' world this story had gained myth status, but the fact that a jeweller was able to perfectly match and mount the missing earring from his stock gems dismisses for all time the widely held view that the keeper's lode were gems new to science.

The stones were crystals of an attractive blue colour; quartz crystals takes their colour from minerals in the host rock and the smoky/yellow cairngorms owe their colours to traces of ferric oxide, the keeper's blue stones were unique in that no blue cairngorms had ever been found. The most likely explanation is that the gamekeeper's lode was not 'cairngorms' at all but kyanite, a sky-blue crystal, recorded in Scotland as having been found quite locally in Glen Tilt, Loch Tay side and also east of Loch Rannoch.

On the great Scottish estates, servants finding anything of note on the ground, be it semi-precious gems or pre-historic carved stones, invariably offered them up to the Big House to appease the Laird.

The keeper at Loch Builg was of sterner stuff; maybe it was because he had no wife and children to think about or maybe his attitude stemmed from his simmering resentment of the head keeper and by association the Laird. We can never tell, but Macpherson the stalker was very much his own man and in time he left Invercauld.

In rural areas there may be much speculation and myths, but very few secrets can be kept from local folk. In towns and villages the public house serves as meeting place and oratory. But Gairnside, with reclusive stone-age characters from the far reaches of the Glen only venturing as far as Ballater once a year to give over their rent to the factor at the Invercauld Hotel, had a more convivial meeting place: the Fit o' Gairn smiddy.

Every farm had horse, and, after the blacksmith at Kirkstyle gave up, Charlie Clark got to know every horse and its master in Glen Gairn.
Charlie told me the story of the 'blue steens'.

'It was efter the first war that Macpherson was at Loch Builg. There was a lang het summer an' abody was short o' water. The crop at Balgairn an' Dalbedgie out on the haugh just came to nithing and withered awa'.

'Word got out about Macpherson's steens fin he left them wi' Albert Thomson's folk at the Post Office. The auld Laird wasna sair pleased but it was ill to get onybody to bide at Loch Builg so he left him aleen'.

'The blue steens came out o' the loch. The stalker fished the loch for the char, the fish were pink fleshed like sma salmon, an' the year o' the low water he stood out on steens that he had niver seen before to get casted faarer o'wer the water. Then he noticed something shining at his feet, an' there was the seam o' blue steens'.

'He could only get at them when the loch was real low, usually at the end o' the summer, an' when a couple years on the steens went deen, he left the Glen'.

CHAPTER 12.

Land of the standing stones

Carn Dearg

If we travel back down Glengairn to the Milton burn, we can follow on foot a Land rover track that climbs steeply up from the road. The Milton burn takes its name from the 'toun' that grew up around an old meal mill here, probably dating from the early 18th.Century. There can still be seen the earthworks of the foundations, and traces of where the burn was diverted to power the mill wheel. But our track today dates only from the 1950s.

We are soon out on the moor above the trees: in a clear day the views up the glen and across to Morven are simply astounding. We can see that the upper Milton burn, now beneath us, divides into east and west branches.

We climb south-east across the broad expanse of hill that separates Glengairn from the Dee valley; at around the 1400 feet level we are walking through an area of many small heaps of stones. Those are clearance cairns gathered off the hill 5000 years ago by the hunter-gatherers to create small areas of level ground to grow grain in their early attempts at farming.

We can find clearance cairns and field systems with their accompanying hut circles all over Upper Deeside. From our present position on the hill, high above and opposite to where the Lary burn joins the Gairn; we can look across to the Craig of Prony. A track winds up through the birch woods from Corrybeg, spiralling clockwise round the hill; this was the road to Glenbardie farm, and again, between 1200 and 1400 feet, you can find the clearance cairns and hut circles as you climb clear of the tree line.

Clearance cairns seen at their best after a heather burn. © Ian Cameron

Glengairn Bronze Age hut circle. © Ian Cameron

Beneath us, again, but further up-river, the Gairn is joined by the Glenfenzie burn; follow this burn upstream, until, just before the A 939 is reached, you will be at an altitude of 1300 feet and could just as easily be back in 2000 BC. The ground here has been farmed for a very long time; the solitary, ruined, farm house still stubbornly displays the date, 1822; that was the year of the building of this last farm house at Glenfenzie and the twilight of a way of life.

There is evidence all around us here of earlier and earlier houses, back to houses with round gables, back to hut circles and back to 2000 BC.

The lime rich ground here has been continuously farmed for at least 5000 years, and it is ironic that the last farm house of 1822, a product of the drive for enclosure and improvement has proved to be the weakest link in a tradition that had survived so long

The last Glenfenzie farmhouse. © Ian Cameron

An exactly similar story is told of Glenbardie farm; there again can be found the evidence of farming going back to hut circles, grain stores, and enclosures, but all set to finish in the face of the improvements that pertained to aid, but, in effect, killed off a sustainable way of life that had survived since the ice went away.

The early farms on Upper Deeside had evolved through the ages; the next photo takes advantage of low evening light to show the furrows of the great wooden 'twelve oxen ploughs' that held sway on Deeside till into the 19th Century. In the same image can be seen the establishment of stone dykes, the stones themselves being the product from clearing the ground from the heather moor. At the top of the picture can be seen the ruins of the croft house and out-buildings and, beyond, the hill. In one quick evening snap, we have revealed a wealth of history, which tells of the toil needed to wrestle one small croft from the Gairnside hills.

Why was that early agriculture being worked so high up on the hills? Simply because the valleys below were still deeply flooded by the granite ridge obstructions downstream, that, acting as a dam and a waterfall, would take millennia to erode and finally drain down the Dee valley. The same process can still be seen active today at the Falls of Muick, where a once much higher barrier extended Loch Muick all the way downstream to the Falls.

Loch Muick once extended all the way down to a much higher falls. © Ian Cameron

Glen Gairn, too, had its own lake; directly below us today the River Gairn encounters the hard rock of Candacraig Hill and changes course by 90 degrees to flow south to the Dee. Many, many years ago at this narrowest part of the valley the glacial debris trapped behind the last link of granite between the Carn Dearg and Candacraig Hill formed a high dam, very similar to what we have seen at Cambus o' May. That impounded lake stretched all the way back upstream to Daldownie.

Old Railway Bridge, uplifted with the line, from the crossing of the Gairn at Balgairn and re-erected over the Gairn here at Daldownie. © Ian Cameron

This cataract, again, took millennia to erode down enough to give us the drainage system we see today. The parallel roads marking the reducing levels of the lake are not obvious until beyond Gairnshiel, but further evidence of the longevity of this expanse of water is afforded by the bed of diatomite found beneath the present-day peat in upper Glengairn.

The diatomite takes the form of a white/grey material; it originated in the deposition of the skeletons of tiny diatoms on the floor of a fresh-water-lake: when the water receded, the deposition turned to the mineral, diatomite. Those deposits were soon covered by blanket peat, under which it is found today.

Large-scale mining of diatomite beds took place near Dinnet up till the First World War; the material was used as a filler material in nitro-glycerine. The peat moss area where the diatomite was found would have originally been under a great expanse of fresh water, now all drained away, leaving only the fossil lochs of Davan and Kinord.

The Kieselguhr diatomite plant on Dinnet Moor. © Ian Cameron

Up here on the shoulder of Carn Dearg we are in the midst of a Neolithic settlement that 5000 years ago would have been on an island with a shoreline of lakes (*See colour plate 28*).

The people would have had boats carved from great logs and they would have had an abundance of fish to catch. We can state this with great authority; only nine miles west is Loch Builg, another fossil, land-locked loch from the last ice-age, which carries a stock of Arctic char to this day.

The early people would have been very aware of their skyline; the southwest looked straight into the ridge of Lochnagar, and to the southeast could be seen the magical pyramidal form of Mount Keen and in the cold north-east rose Morven. On examination, every hut circle has an opening that faces the southwest and the sun.

Apart from days of low cloud, Lochnagar was always there, a place of mystical symbolism, that could even portray a stag's head in its corries.

The founding father of their settlement was head of the power structure; chief of the village and head priest combined, and it was from him that direction was sought in organising time, labour, the planting of their crops, and in general living in harmony with nature. That could be achieved only by strict controls that were soon regarded as sacred, and with this discipline the success of the new agrarian society was assured.

The Stag's Head and Antlers on Lochnagar. © Ian Cameron

Lochnagar's early snow. © Ian Cameron

To control their own destiny truly, the settlement people had to grasp the concept of time and seasons. That was difficult, and, as winter set in, the days grew shorter, the nights became longer and colder, and the sun was lower in the sky every day.

Then the early snows came, dusting Lochnagar first, but soon covering Carn Dearg; with the cold and frost and the ever shorter day-light came the questions: Was this the end of their world? Would the light and warmth disappear altogether?

Those fears afflicted early man everywhere, and in the Mediterranean were countered with light from burning oil; oil that had been pressed from the fruit of the olive tree of Biblical times.

Fast-track forward from 2000 BC to March 1920; Alex Keiller, laird of all Morven estate, had returned from World War One. He sold all his holdings in James Keiller and Son Ltd, the family business, and came north to his estate with one of the first aeroplanes seen on Deeside. Alex Keiller had learnt to fly in the Royal Flying Corps, but he wrecked so many planes, culminating in crash landing in the Seine, that he was invalided out.

That aeroplane used the only level ground around, at Bridge of Gairn farm, for a runway. He amused himself at first by terrifying his female passengers until they absolutely refused to go near the plane. Then he started flying over Morven and the grouse moors; what he saw from the sky set him on a life-long quest as an amateur archaeologist.

Alex Keiller saw prehistoric man's field systems, clearance cairns, enclosures and hut circles. He saw Iron Age forts, barrows and cairns, henges and covered ways, ley lines before they had even been identified as such, and at the top of Corrybeg re-entrant saw, from the sky, a widely spaced circle of stones with a central cairn. This was the Corrybeg Circle; and, what he found there, more than anything else, changed his life (*See colour plate 27*).

The Corrybeg Circle has neither a recumbent stone nor flanker standing stones; instead for alignment it uses the skyline of Lochnagar.

The first winter that Margaret and I spent at Abergairn was hard; the days got shorter and shorter, and colder and colder, the frost held up for weeks. We could sense prehistoric man's primeval fear, in spite of central heating and modern insulation. The frosts gave us clear afternoon skies; a snow-covered Lochnagar was outlined sharply in the bitterly cold air of the afterglow.

As the shortest day approached, we watched the sun setting ever earlier and more easterly until it set in the middle ridge of Lochnagar. That ridge is bounded at each end with higher peaks, and completely out of the blue, the truth hit me.

The next afternoon, around 3pm and the mid-winter solstice, saw me 300 feet above Abergairn at the Corrybeg Stone Circle. It was beyond a magic moment, it was primeval, awe inspiring, and frightening. I stood, freezing, in the centre of a stone circle that had been erected by prehistoric man at least 4000 years before, and I watched the mid-winter sun set on the recumbent ridge of Lochnagar, mid-way between two peaks or flankers. The alignment of the circle pointed me straight at the setting sun. I never felt closer to prehistoric man, I was sharing his discovery, and it was truly uncanny.

Prehistoric Glengairn man had set up the stone circle to mark and observe the setting mid-winter sun on the ridge of Lochnagar, midway between two peaks; the next day the sun would set farther west with a slightly higher arc. Prehistoric man now had a reference point where the sun set on the shortest day; thereafter the days gradually became longer and warmer. That bench mark, giving them the ability to foretell mid-winter, carried great power and so equipped, the tribe flourished. Time passed, and then the glacial ice melt suddenly accelerated as the last of the glaciers disappeared with great quantities of ice melting over the high Cairngorms.

This is to digress within a digression: but, could this great flood have been precipitated by the climate change that caused a great outpouring of fresh water into the Atlantic from Canada, raising sea levels, swamping the land that linked Britain to Europe and ultimately destroying the land bridge between the Black Sea and the Med., hatching the Biblical Noah's Ark story? The date of 2344 BC given to the Biblical flood runs uncannily true for the evidence here on Deeside. More recent research into historic elm tree decline have given a date of 2850 BC as being a time of significant change, to the degree of being an academic boundary between the Mesolithic and the Neolithic, and allowing for the imprecision of radiocarbon dating, this reinforces my argument.

The melt-down resulted in vastly increased run-off that broke through the natural obstructions on the Dee, Gairn and Muick river systems in scenes reminiscent of the Dambusters' breaching of the German dams in WW2. This flooding created, roughly, the drainage pattern of the Dee upper valley that we see today.

Evidence of that final violent torrent can be seen in section on the eroded north bank of the River Dee opposite Deecastle. The top five-metre layer of rough boulders that arrived in the flood sits on top of the earlier glacier-fashioned boulder clay in unconformity.

Five metres of debris as evident opposite Deecastle. © Ian Cameron

Wherever Castle Plant digs in upper Deeside, it finds that same up to five metres of rough post-glacial debris.

Prehistoric man had by then gained the Bronze Age culture, and the drained-down lake floors gave him vastly more level ground, and more fertile ground to expand his farming, and an even more fertile hunting ground on the newly exposed high ground for the minerals, crucial to his culture.

In a short time he ventured into the Howe of Cromar, the Vale of Alford, the fertile lands around Insch and Inverurie. The only thing missing and central to his culture was the skyline of Lochnagar, to regulate seasons, and indeed now, religion and culture.

There again, a genius appeared and set about recreating the skyline of Lochnagar. That was done by building Recumbent Stone Circles.

A classic recumbent stone circle at Keig, Donside. © Ian Cameron

Those circles appear only in the North East of Scotland: each has its large recumbent stone set in the south-west of the circle, flanked by two tall standing stones. The terms: 'Recumbent Stone' and 'Flankers' were coined by our restless amateur archaeologist, Alexander Keiller, F.G.S., F.S.A. The many Recumbent Stone Circles, widely distributed throughout the North East, are built with the Recumbent Stone in the same South-West orientation as viewed from the centre of the Circle, and, if you visit these circles in mid-winter, you will find the sun setting over the great Recumbent, as it was doing on Lochnagar as viewed from the Corrybeg Circle (*See colour plate 29*).

In kinder climes we find ancient temples also aligned to the sun, but not the setting sun; on Gozo, an island off Malta, the rising sun's first rays are aligned to enter the chambers of a gigantic structure built to represent a recumbent woman. The ancients' aim was to represent the union of the Sun and Mother Earth. Here survival took second place to fertility.

There is little doubt that here in the cold North-East of Scotland the Recumbent Stone Circles were set up as indicators of Mid Winter, observing the location of the sun's last and lowest rays from the south-west on the shortest day. This was vital knowledge, linked not to extravagance, status nor ceremony, but simply survival.

CHAPTER 13.

Tomnaverie stone circle

Perhaps the nearest complete Recumbent Stone Circle to Corrybeg is at Tomnaverie just outside Tarland. Tomnaverie: 'The hill of Worship or Justice'. This hill lies to the immediate west of the B9094 at (NJ 486035).

Tomnaverie Stone Circle has had a chequered career; all North-East Scotland Recumbent Stone Circles have suffered over their 4500 year existence. The ravages of weather and time took their toll, but, as they were held in respect and fear by the farming descendents of their original Early Bronze Age constructors, the great stones suffered little physical destruction until the 18th Century and the time of the agricultural improvements. The ready supply of stone was used to build dykes, drains and farm buildings and only the most ponderous of the monoliths were left intact.

Tomnaverie's site survived this phase only to be quarried for road stone from the late 1800's. By the 1920's a huge slice had been removed from the Circle's hill, but our Alexander Keiller, becoming aware of the situation when the blasting felled the flanker stones and caused others to drop into the quarry, lobbied his fellow lairds to get Lord Aberdeen, the landowner, to stop the quarrying. After a heated meeting on site in 1927 the monument was taken into the care of the early Ministry of Works and today, Historic Scotland (*See colour plate 30*).

Fast forward to 1999, the Mac Robert Trust now owned the ground and an enlightened Trust Manager and Factor started to talk to Historic Scotland about restoring Tomnaverie, the fallen stones were still left as they were when the quarrying stopped in 1927.

Two courses of action were decided on.

First Reading University would be asked to undertake a complete excavation and reconstruction of the circle. This work was done over two springs in 1999 and 2000 under the direction of Professor Richard Bradley and his team.

The second course of action was to rebuild the hill by using inert landfill as it became available. Castle Plant (Deeside) Ltd. was chosen for this work, so here I have to declare an interest.

The intention was, on completion, to have a rebuilt Recumbent Stone Circle sitting on top of its hill as it would have appeared 4500 years ago.

There are many, many Recumbent Stone Circles in North-East Scotland, and, as you journey around, their sites become almost monotonous in their predictable. The ancients always sought out a hilltop that commanded an unrestricted view of both the sky and the horizon.

At Tomnaverie there is the, now protected, war time bunker, built close to the Circle, where the local unit of the Royal Observer Corps carried out their search for enemy aircraft during the Second World War, sharing this hill's great view point with the ghosts of the ancients. Indicating perhaps, how little has changed in 4500 years. As Prof. Richard Bradley told me: 'Never think of those people as primitive, they had all the reasoning powers and mental capacity of folks today.'

The work of infilling the hill goes on, after ten years it is almost complete. Prof. Richard Bradley's work is long completed; his is the most recent and comprehensive excavation of a Recumbent Stone Circle, and, if you can find a copy, his 2005 book, 'The Moon and the Bonfire' is the most up to date and revealing of all reports on our Circles.

In summary, he allows to the oldest circles being found in Cromar and Donside, i.e. nearest to Corrybeg. He also hints at a connection between Recumbent Stone Circles and the landscape, i.e. the skyline.

Richard Bradley's findings are mainly concerned with Tomnaverie; significantly, it is the only Recumbent Stone Circle to share Lochnagar's summit ridge's setting sun with Corrybeg on the shortest day of the year.

CHAPTER 14.

Minerals galore

Carn Dearg

I keep digressing, but let us now carry on to the top of Carn Dearg. From that point we look down on the Dee valley; we are 1000 thirsty feet above Coilacriech Inn, and way beyond the tree line. The striking feature around us is the abundance of white rocks. The source of all that quartz is a vertical vein that outcrops across the ridge. That madre de oro ('mother of gold') of the Spanish miners is an impressive sight. They say that if you find gold in situ you will recognise it immediately, and once smitten with gold fever you never recover (*See colour plate 31*).

The extraordinary features of that vein are two-fold. One is its massive width of up to 25 feet in places. The other is that, unlike other veins we have examined where the minerals are enclosed within the host rock, the vein stands proud, like a wall. The host rock has eroded away, but the more resistant quartz is left, naked and vertical until it succumbs to wind and gravity and sections collapse, scattering white quartz debris across the ridge.

The intersecting veins and the depression continuing under the peat, as viewed from the top of the Shenval on the A939. © Ian Cameron

Those structures stretch for over one hundred yards roughly due north; they then appear to be intersected by another series of veins that approaches at 90 degrees. All that activity can be observed from the main A939 road from the top of the Shenval. From that view point, it can be seen that the great north-bearing quartz reef (to give it an Australian name) continues north, not as a reef or dyke, but as an obvious depression on the hillside. It would appear that the structure continues beneath the peat and heather cover for several more hundred yards till it reaches the head waters of the Milton Burn.

Picture taken from same spot, note how the snow accentuates the line of the depression. © Ian Cameron

The quartz is far from barren; all the debris contains a network of smaller veins, crystals, large and tiny, clusters of citrine, evidence of barytes and beryl with silicified quartz of both wine and yellow (*See colour plate 35*).

There are sections of the vein's host granite wall and other sections of greisens, granite that had been altered by contact with the older rocks now all mixed up in this soup of minerals (*See colour plate 32*).

You can see quartz with empty cubic sockets where the iron pyrite crystals had been before they had dissolved over time and many, many winters' rain, frost and snow (*See colour plate 33*).

We can only speculate as to how early Deeside man interacted with those minerals. In Cornwall, granitic greisens were a known source of tin; is this scattered mineral vein debris all that remains of a greater hoard after prehistoric man had salvaged his ingredients for smelting bronze, and recovering the gold? We can never know, but early man did live on these hills, and there is no denying the mineral evidence on top of Carn Dearg.

CHAPTER 15.

Spoils of the Coyles

The Coyles of Muick

"The Coyles of Muick are big and braw, But they are afa' cauld when they are covered with snaw." By a local poet A.Mackie.

On the south side of the Dee lie the Abergeldie and Strath Girnoc hills, and nearer home, the three peaks that make up the Coyles of Muick and the western backdrop to Ballater.

Only the hill on the left with the cairn is the Coyles; Craig of Loinmuie is the hill in the centre and farther away and to the right is Meall Dubh, (the black lump). The Coyles and Craig of Loinmuie are both, surprisingly, of serpentine rock, while Meall Dubh is of meta-basic, massively altered igneous rock.

When you climb to the top of the Coyles, you find a second summit a little farther west, and out of sight of Ballater. The whole area is one of grass land growing on strange cinnamon- brown weathered rock.

There is a certain well-frequented aura to this place; people have been drawn here for a very long time, and it was this sense of antiquity and mystery that drew Alexander Keiller here in 1923.

Flushed with his successful ascent of Morven Hill in his Citreon-Kegresse halftrack, the 'Caterpillar' of local legend, Alexander Keiller turned his attention to new challenges. He combined his archaeological interests with his motor mountaineering and next drove the 'Caterpillar', laden with picks, shovels and strong labourers, to the top of the Coyles.

Alex Keiller in his 'Caterpillar'. © permission Sheila Potter

Keiller surveyed and supervised an archaeological dig on the Coyles; culminating in burying a sealed tin containing his findings and a set of the then current (1923) coins of the realm, including, I was told by one of his labourers, a gold sovereign.

Meall Dubh

Meall Dubh (the black lump) is well named. It is noted as being a home for adders, but on its east face there is a quarry, and here the dark rock is metamorphosed into slates. This Meall Dubh quarry was the source, in the 1700s', of the thick, heavy slates that roofed the original Birkhall House, previously known as Sterin (*See colour plate 36*).

There is no cart road through the hill to Meall Dubh quarry, and the many tons of slate must have been brought down to Birkhall with pack horses rented, no doubt, from the same worthies that normally used their ponies to cart the whisky kegs over the mountains to Angus.

The Craig of Loinmuie

The Craig of Loinmuie is the central and nearest of our three hills: like the Coyles, it is of serpentine rock. The ridge of serpentine has been classified as a SAC (Special Area of Conservation) specifically in regard to the alpine plants that bloom there in early summer; the most noted being the Mossy and Yellow Mountain saxifrages.

The mass of serpentine is also interesting for thin veins of chrysotile filling the fractures in the rock. That fibrous, opaque mineral is similar to the much more valuable Tiger's Eye found mainly in South Africa.

A croft at the back of Craig of Loinmuie. © Ian Cameron

Craig of Loinmuie rises steeply above the land of Loinmuie, once rich pasture that had been farmed since the ice went away. The ground slopes gently up from the Muick, is south-facing, and the serpentine rock broke down into a rich clay, that, despite its great altitude, grew better crops than the light gravel soils of the river terraces downstream could ever achieve.

The hillside was dotted with the crofters' small blackhouses with clay floors, small windows, a kail-yard and a heather-thatched roof. The old folk had picked their home with great care; this was a special place, where, far to the east, they could see the magic peak of Bennachie.

As with the other glens, continuous cultivation could be traced back to Neolithic times: this sustainable existence broke up with the 'improvements' and the application of rents. The improvements brought the building of new granite and slate farm houses and rents; rents that drove the heart out of the people, together with gamekeepers who restricted the age-old right of a fish from the river and a beast from the hill, and foresters who cut off the supply of sticks and stones from the woods. It was that new way of life that was unsustainable.

One by one, the crofts were amalgamated into larger and larger units as the old folk left or died, until finally, there was only one Loinmuie Farm left. The laird built the last Loinmuie Farm house; it was a modern house for its time, the granite stone was brought up from Ballater, it boasted the first and last slated roof on Loinmuie hill and the old kail-yard was enlarged into a wall-enclosed garden, but by 1887 the farm was abandoned.

By 1919, most of the Deeside hills were bare of trees; the Great War and the immense requirements of timber to shore up the miles of trench warfare had taken a brutal toll of the stands of local pine; there was a crisis, and, out of the realisation that timber was a strategic resource, was born the Forestry Commission. The fledgling Forestry Commission's brief was simply to create a reserve of timber for the next war.

That was commendable, but to grow trees, the Forestry Commission first needed land. The whole project seemed to be about to stall for want of ground; in Scotland, land was everything to the lairds; it was their heritage, their traditional powerbase, and it was their duty to hand it on in better heart.

But wars, and winning wars, was also the trade of lairds, and to start the ball rolling King George V gave the embryonic Forestry Commission a long lease on his Allt Cailleach Forest that included the Birkhall sawmill and the farm lands of Loinmuie. Over the next few years the Loinmuie fields were planted

Loinmuie. © Ian Cameron

with conifers. The trees throve on the rich soil and all trace of past human existence disappeared.

Fast forward to the early 1990s: by this time Allt Cailleach Forest had reverted to the Royal Family and it was decided time to clear fell the block of spruce growing on Loinmuie.

Older houses yet with rounded gables. © Ian Cameron

As the trees were cleared a 'Brigadoon' village appeared; the last Loinmuie farmhouse stood again in the sunlight, the previous farmhouse going back to the early 1700s' reappeared, the byres, the well, the long houses, the black houses, older houses yet with rounded gables, and traces of Bronze Age hut circles all came back into being.

The fields have been replanted again with trees and soon our Brigadoon will go back to sleep for another 100 years, but for the present Loinmuie holds court to all who would visit.

CHAPTER 16.

Minerals, monuments and man

In this little book I have culled gently on my knowledge of the immediate surroundings of my home. I describe the rocks and the minerals they hold, and how man has used (and exploited) the resources to improve his lot.

We can trace how early man's superstitions and culture were shaped by natural phenomena and seasonal patterns, and how Early Bronze Age man built the first Recumbent Stone Circles that soon covered the whole of the North East of Scotland. We can see how inter-dependent sustainable living with nature had been, and also see how fragile this arrangement proved to be with the advent of 'enclosure' and 'improved' farming practices and the emergence of sporting estates.

We can see the profound effect that the arrival of the railway at Ballater precipitated. It heralded an end to local limestone quarrying and large-scale peat cutting. The English lime and Welsh coal that came conveniently to every station certainly gave the communities economies in time and labour, but, ironically, time and labour they had in abundance. The lime and coal had to be paid for and it was the money that was in short supply.

This sudden introduction of capitalism into a world where sustainability, community spirit and barter had reigned for so long was a step too far, and too soon.

In the first half of the 1800's, from the time of the Napoleonic Wars, farming had thriven in the glens with rising grain and beef prices; we learn, again and again, of farmers that had made enough money to be able to retire, "doon to Ballater" to build their retirement homes, and name the new houses after their old farms.

Look at Ballater houses; called: Lary, Glenbardie and Loinmuie to this day. Yet a bare 20 years after the railway reached Ballater, the farms of Glenbardie, Loinmuie and Glen Fenzie like countless others lay derelict. True, cheap wheat from the prairie lands of Canada and the U.S. were coming here and agricultural prices were falling, but the goods trains steaming into Ballater put paid to the small Deeside hill farms as surely as the bell of American, cow-catcher embellished, wood burning engines tolled the demise of the buffalo and native Indians on the North American plains.

The railways did create a boom in Ballater house building and brought the embryonic tourist trade, but at the same time accelerated the depopulation of all the side glens.

Perhaps I have strayed beyond my brief, but, as so often happens, one delves into a subject and the findings ask: 'Why?' The searching for the 'whys' then becomes, for me, the most enjoyable and revealing of tasks, and it is hoped will prove so to the reader also.

I trust you will forgive me for side-tracking among the trees, my special places, the smiddy, war-time logging camps and the Neolithic. But I cannot apologise; my love is for all the multi facets of this gem that is my native land, and the discovery, of how intricately every aspect of nature is inter-related, fills me with wonder and humility.

On the mineral front, the creation of sporting estates spelt the end of lead mining in Upper Deeside, the work at the Abergairn mine in the 1870s by Cornish miners was the last recorded. The creation of the Cairngorms National Park Authority ensures that this situation will not easily change in the foreseeable future.

Yet, recent survey work has revealed huge reserves of barytes above Loch Callater at Coire Loch Kander, and, interestingly, signs of much earlier mining there, certainly not for barytes but the accompanying lead. This corrie has been noted for its alpine plants for over 200 years, and the fact that they can only survive because of the underlying geology bears out my premise of the inter-dependency of nature. But a nature left to its own devices; I cannot subscribe to man's interference in ecosystems that have lived in harmony since the ice went away.

To set the record straight; I am not an academic, and, more importantly, I have no pretensions in that direction. Nor do I have an academician's access to either funding or radiocarbon dating, with its associated laboratory and institutional support.

My central aim is to share my knowledge of the minerals all around us, a joyful study that has taken me to very special places and occupied more of my life than I will ever admit.

My thesis on the origin and subsequent spread of Recumbent Stone Circles touches on the basic human hopes and fears that ultimately inspires religion; and the analogy from the recent past that comes to mind is the construction of the Free Church kirks that mushroomed up in every parish after the Disruption of 1843.

A very amateur study, unrestricted by disciplines, deadlines nor budgets; driven only by my love of the wild places and the curiosity of a mind that will not be stilled.

Finally, I can only repeat now, what has been said before, in the words of the Canadian Lumberjack/soldiers who told anyone that would listen in 1942:

"This whole bloody place is moving with minerals!"

Appendix 1.

Recent discoveries

'Abergairn' 1st September 2013.
Our knowledge of the disciplines of geology and archaeology keep advancing with each new discovery and technological development. On our own parochial level, two new discoveries came this year to enrichen our heritage.

First was the unearthing of an early Celtic cross at Tullich Kirkyard in the spring.

7th Century AD Celtic Cross, Tullich Kirkyard. © Ian Cameron

Johnny Simpson with his 6000 year old stone axe head. © Ian Cameron

The second was brought about by a conversation in the Post Office with my friend from schooldays, Johnny Simpson. Johnny said: 'Have you seen my stone-age axe head?' I had not, but by afternoon I had it captured on film.

The story goes: In the late 1940's workmen were building Ballater's post-war council houses. A digger driver had occasion to visit our local doctor, Sir George Middleton. At the surgery they got talking and the driver told Sir George of finding the stone axe head. The doctor was an avid collector of archaeological artefacts and he was given the stone axe head.

Many years later whilst on a visit south to Sir George's daughter, Johnny Simpson was gifted the axe head in order for it to be returned to its place of finding in Ballater.

Index

Abergairn 12, 13, 17, 19, 20, 30, 31, 54, 58, 61, 77, 78, 90.
Abergeldie Castle 18.
Adam Welfare vi.
Agates 15, 16, 17.
Allt Cailleach 45, 87.
Amethyst 26, 47.
Arrowhead 67.
Artic Char 75.
Ballater 9, 10, 11, 12, 13, 16, 17, 18, 23, 24, 25, 26, 31, 32, 35, 36, 37, 39, 41, 44, 45, 46, 51, 53, 54, 61, 66, 67, 70, 85, 87, 89, 90.
Balmenach 12.
Balquhain 27.
Barytes 54, 84, 90.
Beryl 23, 26, 84.
Bob Shaw 65, 66, 67.
British Geological Survey 19, 23, 61.
Bronze 19, 61, 62, 63, 66, 67, 72, 79, 81, 84, 88, 89.
Cairngorms 16, 29, 46, 55, 69, 78, 90.
Canadians 32, 91.
Candacraig 74.
Carn Dearg 71, 74, 75, 77, 83.
Charlie Clark 17, 18, 53, 70.
Circle of Auchmaliddie 27.
Citreon-Kegresse 85.
Citrine 12, 84.
Coilacreich Inn 83.
Coire Loch Kandar 90.
Copper 16, 61, 62, 63, 64.
Corrybeg Stone Circle 21, 71, 77, 78, 80, 81, 82.
Coyles of Muick 36, 85.
Craig of Loinmuie 85, 86.
Creag - an - t-seabhaig vii, 9, 12, 13, 30.
Creag Phiobaidh 13.
Daldownie 74.
Dalnabo 55, 56.
Diatomite 74.
Disruption 91.
Dr Heddle 15, 47, 55.
Elvan dyke vii, 20, 21.
European Larch 55, 56.
Felspar 21.
Flint 46, 66, 67.
Fluorite 19, 20, 23.
Francis Farquharson 23, 24, 30, 36, 37, 39.
Gabbros 11, 12, 47.
Gairnshiel 61, 63, 74.
Garnets 44, 55, 56, 59.

Glacial ice-melt 9, 50, 74, 78, 79.
Glen Fenzie 19, 65, 89.
Glenbardie 71, 72, 89.
Gold 12, 16, 19, 63, 67, 83, 86.
Goza, Malta 80.
Huntly 18, 20, 24.
Hut Circles 11, 67, 71, 72, 77, 88.
Invercauld 25, 70.
Iron 12, 15, 19, 33, 47, 48, 49, 50, 62, 63, 64, 77, 84.
Iron Pyrites 12.
John Betjeman 26.
Keig Stone Circle 80.
Keiller 18, 27, 65, 77, 80, 81, 85, 86.
Kiln 10,11, 13, 14, 57, 58, 59, 66.
King George V 18.
King James' 50.
Kyanite 69.
Lary 71, 89.
Lead 12, 13, 16, 17, 18, 19, 30, 31, 32, 33, 44, 45, 90.
Legends of the Braes O' Mar 50.
Limestone 11, 13, 15, 44, 48, 49, 55, 56, 57, 58, 59, 89.
Lithium 23.
Loch Builg 69, 70, 75.
Loch Callater 90.
Loch Ullachie 13.
Lochnagar 36, 51, 75, 77, 76, 78, 80, 82.
Lord Byron 36, 45.
Macpherson 70.
Meall Dubh 85, 86.
Migvie 50.
Monaltrie House vi, 9, 23, 24, 25, 36.
Morven vii, 9, 11, 12, 16, 18, 36, 41, 45, 47, 48, 49, 65, 66, 67, 71, 75, 77, 85.
Newfoundlanders 9, 10, 35, 39.
Pannanich 9, 35, 36, 37, 39, 40, 44, 45, 51.
Pass of Ballater 9, 13, 23, 24, 25, 26, 31, 36, 45, 54, 61, 67.
Peat 11, 41, 48, 65, 66, 67, 74, 84, 89.
Platinum 16.
Poseidon 16.
Prince of Wales 18.
Prof. Richard Bradley 82.
Quartz 12, 17, 21, 26, 27, 28, 29, 40, 43, 46, 56, 59, 69, 83, 84.
Serpentine 85, 86.
Silver 12, 16, 19, 23, 26, 30, 32, 45, 63.
Smiddyhill 50.
Snow Tower 26.
Tin 61, 62, 86.
Tom an Lagain 13.
Tullich Kirk 9, 39.
Tungsten 16, 54.
Wattie Muir 16.

Notes

ND - #0098 - 060826 - C16 - 234/156/5 - PB - 9781780356990 - Gloss Lamination